did i
say
that
out
loud?

did i say that out loud?

Notes on the chuff of life

Fi Glover & Jane Garvey

First published in Great Britain in 2021 by Trapeze,
an imprint of The Orion Publishing Group Ltd
Carmelite House, 50 Victoria Embankment
London EC4Y 0DZ

An Hachette UK Company

1 3 5 7 9 10 8 6 4 2

A CIP catalogue record for this book is
available from the British Library.

ISBN (Hardback) 978 1 3987 0566 1
ISBN (Export Trade Paperback) 978 1 3987 0567 8
ISBN (eBook) 978 1 3987 0569 2
ISBN (Audio) 978 1 3987 0570 8

Typeset by Input Data Services Ltd, Somerset

Printed and bound in Great Britain by Clays Ltd, Elcograf S.p.A.

www.orionbooks.co.uk

FROM JANE:
TO EVELYN AND SIAN

FROM FI:
TO HECTOR AND HONOR

CONTENTS

AUTHORS' NOTE

If you've heard our podcast, you can probably imagine the meetings we had about this book. Long, meandering, disappearing up conversational cul-de-sacs, usually going nowhere, sometimes weirdly entertaining. How could we attempt to recreate, in book form, a podcast in which two women exchange random thoughts, occasional pleasantries, fatuous double-entendres, real-life challenges and often sudden bursts of something approaching wisdom?

While some of the great media beasts can delight us with a book a year, we always seemed to have excuses . . . or reasons . . . for why we couldn't get started. Too busy. Too many teenagers. Too tired. Too scared. And then, well, you know what happened. A pandemic struck the world and no one could leave their homes. There was no real excuse not to get on with something. It turns out there was stuff we hadn't said, after all. And now we had time to say it. Like a lot of people, we both felt the need to keep our minds busy in order to fill the anxiety void with something. A lot of this book is about everything we're still trying to fathom out. We're experts in nothing, despite both thinking we knew it all not that long ago. Which is odd.

We have written this book in the closest thing we could get to conversational form, so one of us writes a chapter and the other one responds to it. If we'd tried to write as we actually speak it would have looked like a Year 7 drama class gone wrong, and we'd also be interrupting each other all the time. Absolutely nothing in this book is an attempt by either of us to tell anyone how to live. It is not a bible for midlife. Nor is it meant to be an incendiary literary device. We both try to acknowledge and understand our own privilege, because we know that not everyone gets to write a book. And if at times you think you can do better – well, we are kind of with you on that . . .

You don't have to agree with a word we've written, by the way. We might have changed our minds too by the time you get to the end of any given chapter. But that is the fabulous art of female conversation. We are all practitioners of it, but by no means qualified in it.

So, basically, pop this between your ears and give it a shake-around if you fancy. If you don't, simply bung it in the regifting drawer. Just remember not to give it back to us, please.

Fi and Jane

I

HARK AT HER:

MIDLANDS MOTELS
AND JUDGING

JANE

YOU LEARN TO PASS JUDGEMENT long before you know you're doing it. Conveniently, the past is littered with women who were no better than they ought to be. Like that so-called saint, Joan of Arc – ideas way above her station. Anne Boleyn? A right piece of work. Marie Curie – no doubt her lab work was commendable, but there's photographic evidence she had an issue with flyaway hair.

We like to think we're better than that now, but try sticking your head above the twenty-first-century parapet and see what happens. Express an opinion, state a fact, be yourself . . . it's dangerous stuff. You're asking for trouble.

In my 1970s adolescence, the No Better Than They Ought To Be's were everywhere you looked. We even had one or two in our street. They weren't astride the national stage, these women, they were brazenly living their lives in the suburban North of England. Back then it wasn't always obvious to me how they'd strayed from the path of righteousness exactly, although I knew enough to understand that a serious commitment to fags and bottle-blonde hair might well be indicators – clues that something was not quite 'right'.

These ne'er-do-wells were certainly all over our very small telly, too; cheeky staples in costume dramas, heavily corseted with full, heaving bosoms and rouged cheeks, wisps of straw still in their golden tresses, as though they'd popped up for air after a rural romp. Every one of these shows seemed to me to be set in Cornwall. Or on the high seas. Or on the high seas just off Cornwall. And everything was firmly at some unspecified point in days of Yore, a time when men strutted about in breeches inspecting things with their hands behind their backs and women said, 'Oh master', and nine months later a nervy housemaid was dispatched to get the hot water and towels.

Fast forward to the advent of *The Brothers*, risky peak-time Sunday-night fare about battling Brummie siblings running a haulage company. The glamour! No bosomy wenches here, but a fair few low-cut tops in difficult fabrics. Probably no good after the first wash. The Netflix generation, raised on high-octane, glossy entertainment, do not know they're born. Still, 1970s Britain, replete after a traditional roast with a proper hot pud and custard to follow, sat transfixed. As far as I recall, there were no breeches in *The Brothers*, but at least one couple had a very messy divorce. Wine glasses were thrown about. No doubt the fault of the lady, she'd have egged him on. Women did that.

In Soapland, many a plot was driven by the woman in a fake-fur coat with attitude to spare and what we all knew to be the burden of a 'reputation'. Men didn't have reputations. Or if they did, they were always accompanied by a woman saying, 'Oh, don't mind him! It's just his way!'

Lots of the female characters in *Coronation Street* had reputations, but my early favourite was Vera from *Crossroads*. If you weren't around at the time, you'll need to be armed with some basic information about the show and a willingness to suspend your disbelief. Here we go then, and don't say you weren't warned. At a time when I doubt Britain had a single actual motel, *Crossroads* was set in a top, possibly four-star Midlands motel, close to the region's dazzling motorway network. It attracted a range of guests, both shady and sophisticated. It was Vera's fate to be attracted to many of them. And it's fair to say that a good many suitors hopped onboard.

Miss Vera Downend (she would never have been a Ms) was the Crossroads Motel's hairdresser, who lived and loved on a houseboat. Vera – played by the wonderfully named Zeph Gladstone – was a foxy brunette, I should emphasise, but otherwise she exactly fitted the ne'er-do-well bill. Wiki now describes Vera – to my shock – as a 'tart with a heart'. I suppose it's true: Vera's suitors came, and then they went. Sometimes with better hair, because she was a damn good hairdresser. When I got home from school, homework dispensed within thirty minutes or less ('Jane needs to apply herself . . .') I'd immerse myself in the messy affairs of King's Oak, the Midlands. And even my pea-sized brain was receiving some important messages. You could be a Vera. You could live in wacky, alternative, water-based accommodation and have a string of lovers between bubble perms and blue rinses, but chances are you would not find yourself sitting pretty at sixty-five with hubby safely tucked away on the golf course, something unctuous in the slow cooker and the prospect of a couples-only river cruise up the Danube hoving into view.

Oh, these wrong'un women like Vera had spectacular flurries of excitement. Wild peaks of ecstasy, troughs of despair. Brimming with confidence, and sometimes almost predatory, they may – fleetingly – have had a better time than the rest of us, but there was always a price to be paid. They got the candle-lit steak (steak!) dinners and trips away, but you knew there'd be no big white wedding for the saucy minx who led the gent astray. He'd no doubt go on to find lasting happiness with a handily placed local virgin, while the hapless vixen died toothless and alone in a filthy hovel with only her schooner of gin for company. The hovel would definitely be filthy, because women of that sort have very low hygiene standards. If her hovel had a fridge (and I accept it's a big if), she would not bother to clean behind it. My adolescent self was beginning to get it. Women, it seemed, had some choices to make. Do you want to be one of *them*, or one of the other sort? Stuck on your houseboat waiting for a debonair car salesman called Lance or Vince to pluck up the courage to leave his missus, or a contented life in suburbia with a decent, dependable Brian, someone who knew his way around loading a dishwasher? I could be a woman people talked about, or a woman who talked about the women people talked about.

To be fair, the chances of me flouncing through life as any sort of temptress already seemed remote, even in 1980. I think that dream had died the night that year when I saw Debbie Harry fronting Blondie at the Deeside Leisure Centre, standing on tiptoe on soggy squares of carpet on the ice-rink. She was unimaginably beautiful, a pop goddess, simply luminous. I was fifteen, in a Marks and Sparks ski jacket with contrasting dark- and light-blue panelling, squinting because I hadn't wanted Debbie to see me in my NHS glasses. This meant I couldn't really see her very clearly, but I saw enough to know when I was beaten. 'Atomic', 'Union City Blue', 'Heart of Glass'. My fists clenched with both excitement and fear, deep in the pockets of my ski jacket. Now this – *this* was power, and it felt dangerous. Power in a raw, pulsating, uber-female form. Centre-stage, her hands on her hips. Looking us in the eye. Daring us not to be captivated. Power I would never have.

I interviewed Debbie Harry decades later and made a near-total hash of it. I walked into the *Woman's Hour* green room and there she was – by then, very definitely, Deborah Harry. DEBORAH. In dark glasses, looking at her phone. Bored, no doubt, at the prospect of yet another encounter with someone who'd be terrified of her. What do you say to her? Did I tell her about my unforgettable night in 1980? I don't think I mentioned it – I'm pretty sure I just burbled an introduction and I do remember she was somewhat dismissive, only to apologise later in the studio for being rude. It didn't matter, Deborah, dismiss me all you like. I will always be in awe. I remain very much available, should you require someone to de-clag your shower drain or take your pet tarantula for a stroll.

So it was becoming clear: temptresses were taller than me, didn't shop at M&S, tended not to have abundant and unruly mops of hair, and if they were staying up late at night it was for something more exciting than listening to BBC Radio Merseyside's coverage of Liverpool FC's European Cup campaigns. I accepted my fate. I was to become one of the judgers, not the judged.

And it's definitely much easier being in the majority. Much safer. And so much fun! Welcome. You'll like it here. We're never short of entertainment. Always something new. Women just keep on popping up, saying and doing silly things and, frankly, asking for it. That's when we pounce.

It's worth saying that consistency is not required when it comes to casting judgement. Unless you want to be consistently inconsistent – that's fine. There's always been a good journalistic living to be made in Cutting Her Down a Peg or Two, too, if you're prepared to do it.

I know we all admire the scorching wit, the artistry and the courage of the great female writers and columnists who knock the stuffing out of the patriarchy week in, week out. I actually enjoy reading them. But I doubt they earn as much as the women who specialise in the art of building her up, knocking her down and then sticking a fashionable boot in. I enjoy reading them, too.

Don't feel guilty about it! It's only a bit of fun. No one remembers anyway. Well actually, that's not entirely true. Just as I can still picture the face of the reporter who knocked on my door when I was getting divorced and asked, 'Do YOU think they're having an affair?', shamefully, I do recall the newspaper columnists who've said anything about me. I can probably quote exactly what they said. Imagine what it must be like to be forever in their sights, unable to do anything without it being picked apart. So it's wrong to say no one remembers. You'll probably remember if it's about you, I'm afraid.

Still, as every woman knows, we must all develop a thicker skin and move on, as it's our fault for being oversensitive. We can also help ourselves. There are some areas where women and girls continue to go wrong. For a start we persist in going out and about, quite shamelessly in possession of our female bodies (sometimes even after dark, taking our chances, keeping the car keys bunched in our fists).

Occasionally we seek to change those bodies. We may lose or gain weight, for example. This is very dangerous, and a clear provocation to others.

So, you've lost a few pounds of lard. On the one hand, well done. No one likes a big lump of a thing. I imagine you were pretty lazy before, lolling around in front of *Lorraine* on that huge flat-screen telly and gorging on More-Chocolate-than-Biscuit biscuits. Just waiting for the sweet relief of Lambrusco o'clock. So you finally do the decent thing – pop on some sportswear and drag your lumpy carcass around the park a few times. Knock the twenty-three units a week on the head. Limit your carbs. Follow the advice of all the contributors to those 'My Ideal Weekend' supplement features – you know, the loose-limbed miracles, the egg-white omelette and steamed fish brigade. The weight drops off. Slowly at first. But soon you really do start to look 'better', and people comment. Have you reached your 'perfect weight'? Well, bully for you, darling – because now you need to be very careful. Very careful indeed.

Are you looking a bit scrawny? I'm only asking because I'm worried about you. I know it's never good to be carrying extra timber, and you were always on the big side, weren't you ... but really, being thin can be terribly ageing. And you've always looked so youthful! Nothing wrong with a little of what you fancy. Men like something to grab hold of. And who the hell wants to be around some joyless Jessie limiting the parmesan shavings on her rocket salad?

No, far better to be a little chunkier. Come on, ladies, don't deny yourselves – life is for living. May your sirloin always come with thrice-cooked chunky chips. May your syrup tart be laden with a canister of full-strength squirty cream. May your . . . Oh, you get the picture. Enjoy!

But not too much, because then you'll be fat. And fat is wrong. Being fat allows other people to have a view of you. They can lounge on their sofas, watch their very own flat-screen tellies, burp occasionally, scroll on their phones and pass judgement on you as part of a traditional bit of 'me time'. It's relaxing. And we all need to relax, don't we?

Being in shape means you have self-respect. Standards. A woman should also be well groomed, but not to the extent that she seems to be trying too hard. So it's essential to wear make-up, as blemishes, bumps and unattractive redness will alarm decent folk, but it must be applied properly. No one must know. If you have dreadful wrinkles, if your facial features are sagging and droopy, do consider Botox. It's just considerate. Think of others!

Don't have too much Botox, though, because that will make people laugh and they'll point and stare and accuse you of trying to stay absurdly youthful.

Dress fashionably, but beware: if you dress too fashionably, you run the very real risk of being mutton dressed as lamb. And no one wants that. The cut-off point for high fashion is about thirty-one. Perhaps mid-thirties if you've kept yourself in trim.

And, whatever you do, don't get to forty and slide into the elasticated-waist abyss. Where's your self-respect? You don't have to give up on looking stylish, you know.

It's such a shame that so many women seem to get beige and stay there, forever frumpy. Is it any wonder their partners stray?

Oh yes, partners. You must get married. But not too often. Once is preferable. But if there's infidelity, be prepared to stick around. That's absolutely the right thing to do. What, he's done it again? And you're still there? What kind of an example are you setting here? Don't be a doormat. The whole world's laughing at you.

Remember to have children. But not just one. And, crucially, not too many. And absolutely do NOT give them silly names.

Make sure you keep working. It's vital for your self-respect. Get a nanny if you have to.

NEVER neglect your children. What's this about you pursuing your career and leaving someone else to bring up your own flesh and blood?

There are opportunities here – I've been a fool! Let's turn it into a bit of entertainment. Not a return to the stocks or the ducking stool, something much less dreadful. How about the 'Hark at Her Roadshow'? Like the Radio 1 Roadshows of my youth, only without the giveaway biros and the men in too-tight shorts who should know better.

'Hark at Her' could travel the land, park up in a lay-by, and every community could supply women to sit on stage while the crowd had a bloody good go. Chances are they're doing it anyway, so why not in public? Raise a bit of money for a local charity? The lady who'd got a bit above herself. The woman who'd put herself about a bit. The one who'd let herself go. There'd be a host – an older regional TV chap in a novelty bow tie works well in these sorts of situations – and we'd make sure it didn't get out of hand. I'd host it myself, but in truth I'd rather be in the audience. Sitting comfortably, with my tribe. Delighting in the special thrill that only comes with another woman's downfall. Poor thing.

FI

SISTER, SISTER – HOW GOOD it is to hear someone of your calibre admitting to a bit of 'Hark at Her'-ing. I think it's a habit we all have but pretend we don't, like nose-picking, and occasionally just switching off *In Our Time* if it gets a bit dull.

But my first thought on reading this was that I am so envious of you actually seeing Blondie live. So very envious. I worshipped at the Debbie Harry altar, but only from afar. She never graced our rec. Her appearances on *TOTP* are seared into my teenage memory. The way she barely danced, barely smiled, but just radiated. Hers was such a powerful image of beauty and talent, wasn't it?

I'll confess that I don't understand much of what you say about *Crossroads*. We weren't allowed to watch TV after school, not until all homework/flute/oboe practice was done ('Fiona is a very diligent pupil . . .'), but as you

15

have literally three times as many A-Levels as me, you can be the judge of whether that policy worked or not.

We'd hit TV after dinner, so my diet was *Dallas* and *Dynasty* and then *Knots Landing* – the TK Maxx of American soaps. From what you say of the stunning motel on the ring road of modernity, the same themes and memes for women existed, with shoulder pads. Just thinking about the role of Sue Ellen in *Dallas* makes me queasy now. A fragile, beautiful drunk, trapped in a cruel marriage – I hope that these days we'd only see that kind of shit go down in a documentary by Stacey Dooley about coercive control. I hope it wouldn't be considered entertainment. Then there was Pam with her enormo boobs just simpering away at Bobby. And Charlene Tilton, whose nominative determinism meant she literally tilted when she walked because she, too, had enormo boobs. Do you remember Donna? A kind of Wafty Background Woman Without Bosoms – the Nice biscuit in the variety biscuit box. And then we had matriarchal Miss Ellie in all her frumpy tent frocks. As a woman past her sexual sell-by date all she was allowed to do was lay out lots of breakfasts for people on the windy Southfork terrace and pass the orange juice around. Good God, Jane, how did our generation come out of all of that as sharp and independent as we are?

But if we have been raised to look at women just as I have done there – and it is telling that I have rushed to judgement on all of them – how do we train the next generation not to? Is that even possible? Is modern TV encouraging something different? I think the runes are so good and yet so bad. On the one hand we have that family of Kardashians who only wish to be judged. There is no other plot. It is their simple, and well-exploited, reason for being. Their enhanced body shapes alone make me livid – yet I stare at them just like everyone else does. They are the only four women on the planet who look like that – yet about 1 billion kids probably seek to emulate them. You could literally call their TV show 'Hark at Them'.

But, on the other hand, there is so much stuff we watch these days that is healthier than anything seen on the Southfork terrace. Most of our shared household TV-watching is American-sitcom based. British soaps just feel like self-harm. And so we've done *Modern Family*, *The Goldbergs*, *Life in Pieces* and *Black-ish*, and in all of them the women tackle the judgement of other women head on. It's in their scripts and plots all the time, along with themes of bullying and teens being mean and sexuality in flux and all of that – a wonderful mish-mash of non-judgy humour. The moms are portrayed as heroes, but blissfully flawed ones, too. Every single one of them drinks a bit too much wine from time to time (but not so much as to be sad like Sue Ellen), they aren't always comfortable with having curbed their careers for their kids and they find endless joy in affectionately barracking the men they are with.

Is there some comfort to be found in the sheer choice we have on offer to us as viewers and individual commentators now? As we're all hiving off into these separate existences where we don't feel as if there is only one set of people in front of us, is it possible that the narrow gauge of acceptability remains – but there are just lots of gauges? You can have your Kardashians and I'll have my Claire from *Modern Family*, my daughter will have her Billie Eilish and we might all end up a bit happier.

You are so very right to investigate the notion that we only have ourselves to blame. Is it the right time to wheel out the mighty Maya Angelou quote: 'I've learned that people will forget what you said, people will forget what you did, but people will never forget how you made them feel.' I really, really, really want to live this way but . . . on my way out of the door to a night on the town, do I apply myself to thinking of several empathetic ways in which I might make my friends feel fabulous that evening, or do I mostly just check my reflection in the hallway mirror and hope we're off to a low-level lighting venue that won't expose the wrinkles and the chin hair too much? I could pretend it's the former, but it's usually the latter. Although all the outside influences might be allowing us – and positively encouraging us – to indulge our judgemental side, ultimately we all have a choice to suspend judgement. In the moment we choose not to take it.

Oh, and by the way, I did meet Debbie Harry once. We were having our toes done on neighbouring pedicure chairs in a nail bar. She leaned over and said she liked the colour I'd chosen, a dark morello-cherry red. I stared at her as this sentence formed in my head:

'You are one of the most wonderful creatures of sass and voom on this planet, and I can't thank you enough for simply being out front in a band way back in 1980, and then looking after someone you loved – probably at a cost to yourself and your career – and for then coming back and doing your stuff in a tracksuit and not giving a shit and still saying things of merit and writing a searingly honest autobiography with all the horrid stuff about sexual assault in it.'

What I actually managed to say was: 'Would you like to use it too?' while thinking, 'Boy, she looks old.'

Mea effing culpa.

Oh, and how soon can we get the roadshow up and running? That's a genius idea. Can we call it *The XX Factor*?

2

GOOD HAIR DAYS:

SHADERS AND TONERS
AND SELF-DOUBT

FI

CAN WE TALK ABOUT HAIR, PLEASE?

Some people might be able to tell you the story of their lives in albums, or in books, or in landmark world events – I can tell you mine in hairstyles and hair colours. I can date an event against the background of straight or curly, wafty or in between. There has, quite simply, been a lot of hair in my life.

It's taken fifty-two years of follicle adventure to get here, and to save you having to break off to do an image search, 'here' is straight, longish, with a bit of a fringy thing going on and the colour is currently brown. It's not just any old brown though. It's a bespoke dye that comes from a selection of tubes, which is then mixed up and plastered all over my head by Fran, a clever twenty-three-year-old Italian/Essex hair maven at the salon round the corner whom I could not live without, and whom I see more often than my best friend.

Nothing about my hair is natural any more, and just having hair takes up an absurd amount of time. It touches most areas of my life. It governs more than my daily routine. I can't go on holiday to anywhere with more than 60 per cent humidity, and I'd struggle with no electricity supply for the many appliances needed to get it looking right, so camping is out. Rain is problematic for the same reasons. Windy days are to be feared. My hair doesn't move of its own accord – only after applying three different products can it sway gently in a breeze, and if left to dry naturally it resembles spun sugar, and cracks accordingly.

Mine has been a tempestuous love affair with my hair and the industry surrounding it.

It started with 'Sun In' which, as every teenager from the 1980s knows, is the gateway drug to full-on hair abuse. Spray it on and watch as a strange orange gaudiness spreads across your scalp. We were seduced by the name and all it conjured up and, just to reassure you, it does still work in the gloom of an English summer. When we'd dried up our hair enough with the low-level bleach of 'Sun In' there were also the weekly doses of 'Shaders and Toners' – those little sachets of promise available for 79p in Boots or Woolworths. They were perfect entertainment for boring Saturdays in a small market town in Hampshire when you were not brave enough to nick a frosted-pink lipstick. They were meant to be temporary, but they really weren't. We'd go for weeks with strange purple-reddish tints in our hair even if we'd bought ones that claimed to do something blonde. Or 'ash-blonde', as the S&T brand-development team would say. The names of hair colours always made me laugh. Warm amber? Iced chocolate? Copper-gold? These evocative, daring descriptions were full of promise yet unrecognisable as actual colours. Who has ever walked into a room and said, 'Which one is Sharon?' for someone to reply, 'Oh the one over there, with the champagne-gold hair.'

Once we had made our way through this hors d'oeuvre of temporary colours, the time came – around the age of fifteen – for the main course and some permanent statements. I experimented with full-on bleaching for a while, which did not suit either my reddish complexion or the family bath towels. When a pay packet allowed, there were lowlights and highlights and keratin treatments and sitting under hot lamps with foils. I've bought oils to rub in and sprays to wash out. Over the decades I've walked into hairdressers with pictures of Farrah Fawcett and Annie Lennox, expecting both to be achievable. Tired hairdressers have looked at me askance and shaken their heads slowly but firmly in the same way that a bartender in Wetherspoons might if you waltzed in and asked for a dirty martini served with a fresh olive, a twist of lemon and poured over crushed ice in a crystal glass, please. I have had many, many epic hair fails. In my graduation picture my hair is channelling King Charles (the one with the spaniels) with its height and curls. It was 1989, but that is still no excuse. About a year later I look more like the spaniels. I've gone overnight from hair so long you could plait it like a Swedish folk singer to so short you couldn't really see it. As you can imagine, the intervening years are all over the shop. When my first grey hairs arrived I had no qualms or inner conversations with myself – it was simply an excuse to spend even more time and money with The Frans.

And of course I should know better. I've read the Narcissus story in its many different forms throughout my life. I can sing all the words to Carly Simon's 'You're So Vain'. I know that vanity is bad. From an early age we are taught that it rots your core, draws you into the well; it promotes in you a shallow disregard for the more worthwhile pursuits in life, and polishing up its shiny veneer will cost you proper relationships and feelings. I know this message. You know this message. It is there, where all seeds are sown, in our universal childhood.

I was a bit chubby as a kid. Not bounce-me-round-the-room chubby, or tut-at-mum-in-the street chubby (see earlier 'Hark at Her' chapter), but I wasn't svelte. It didn't bother me until around the age of ten, and then suddenly it started to bother me a lot. Being still in the habit of running everything past my lovely mum, I asked her why I was a bit fatter than my older sister. I did this while sitting on my bed of an evening around the time we'd say our prayers. And we did say prayers – every night as kids. We went to church on Sundays and sang in the choir and said grace before meals, and we knew our Bible stories. I liked it all back then, although I don't, in my adult life, subscribe to any faith and my mum doesn't any more either; but if you do and it brings hope and warmth then good for you. I imagine we were doing it for those reasons at the time, too.

Anyway, I remember saying, 'Mum I don't like being chubby, in particular I don't like my legs,' or words to that effect, to which she replied, 'God made you in his own image,' and left it at that.

It was a tad confusing. Even though we lived in a small hamlet in the middle of rural Hampshire and there was no internet to tell me things outside of my own world, I knew that it was unlikely that God had indeed made me to look like Him because that would mean that He looked like me. I hazarded a guess that literally nowhere in the world was there a depiction of God as a ten-year-old with her dad's knees and a rumble of podge across the thighs who was currently sporting some cut-off dark-pink denim shorts and a much-sought-after pair of Abba clogs – yes kids, BRANDED ABBA CLOGS! They were a work of merchandising genius and I had worn my mother down with my endless requests for them. I'm not surprised she'd looked upwards for support. Anyway, I knew that this image simply hadn't caught on across the ceilings of chapels in Rome, or the stained-glass windows in the church up the road or any of the books we sang hymns from at school. Personally, I think the C of E could have done with upgrading the image of the Good Lord from time to time – it seems odd to have Him stuck in just the one style: flowing white robes and the slightly wavy but well-groomed hair. In fact, nowhere in the pictures I had seen from the Bible was there anything other than pleasing imagery of the human body. Every illustrator of Jesus on the cross had quite a thing about abs, none of the disciples were fat. Mary had nice hair considering she'd been on quite a 'journey', and she didn't seem to have put on the pregnancy weight that engulfs many of us later in life.

Don't think I'm being sacrilegious – I am not decrying faith for a moment – but don't you think the artwork that comes out of it could do with being a bit more, er . . . all-embracing?

Back in my ten-year-old world I do know that my mum was just trying to be wise and instil in me a hearty disregard for my own reflection, but it made no sense at all to be told that appearances didn't really count when that clearly wasn't the case. The twin engines of myth were revving up by that age, though, and Mum had backup because the other Exocet missile about to hit me as a young woman was the one that tells us that some-one will 'see' us one day. Someone, somewhere will see through the veneer and they will come to love us 'warts and all' (although, if you do have warts, do get yourself to the clinic). We'll stand in the shadows of the dance floor and our prince or princess will come and take our hand, he/she/they will lead us to a golden future and see us for our wonderful selves. Together we'll waltz past the thinnies on the dance floor on to a life of fulfilled love and happiness. So we mustn't worry – how shallow those vain beauties are, how unfulfilled their lives will be! This message powers through literature – Austen, the Brontës,

George Eliot – all the stuff we were about to start reading at school. Although again, rather confusingly, when any of those big stories of love and life come to the screen, even the plain people are gorgeous.

But you know what these stories are meant to tell us. You know the formula. And, just like a book or a film or a TV show, we become programmed to expect the right resolution. So this should be the point in the chapter when I tell you how the story of my life in hair has reached a climax and how I have finally achieved a sense of maturity, and the realisation that all of my follicle dalliance was shallow and stupid. It should be like the forty-seventh minute in *Death in Paradise* where the Chief has a sudden light-bulb moment, and he looks knowingly into the middle distance as the pieces of the puzzle fall into place. It should be the moment in a *Morse* where he puts on a bit of opera, Lewis shrugs his shoulders, they go for a pint and for a nanosecond all is right in the world again. I *should* be about to reveal to you the sheer relief and pleasure in finally being able to just go grey and to put all of this nonsense and expense and time, not to mention the chemicals and the plastic, behind me.

But I am going to disappoint you. I'm going rogue on your sense of sensibility. I know what I *should* now be doing with my hair at the age of fifty-two. I should be chopping off the age-inappropriate length. I should go for a more 'manageable' style. I should ditch all of the silicone-based frizz-easing products. For heaven's sake, I work in radio. Ours is, thankfully, not an industry where appearances matter. Added to that, I work at Radio 4 – which, as well as being the home of the nation's brain-power, is also the home of bad hair. I love and admire many of my colleagues but, in a line-up, you could identify a Radio 4 native based on their unkempt barnet. Everyone has 'intellectual' hair. Or maybe my colleagues just don't have combs.

So this is not how my story ends. This hair story ends in an absurd determination to just keep going with the fakery. I'd love to be an old woman with absurdly obvious dyed hair. I reserve my right to be the daftest brush in the cupboard, rocking in my chair in the warm conservatory of the BBC Retirement Home for the Impartial and Infirm with a pelt of sleek and glossy brown hair, which couldn't possibly be mine. I don't want to go grey. I don't want to stop 'doing' my hair. Since the demise of my short-lived crafting period (2006 to 2007, I blame the hormones of childbirth) I think it is the closest thing I have to a hobby. And I'd like to end this paean to the art of hair in the way that all lessons in life should end, with a dedication to those who have paved the way before me.

Three of my favourite women in journalism have given me the courage of my convictions. No less than Emily Maitlis, Joan Bakewell and Nora Ephron. I know. Legends, all of them.

They are women who are bolder and more assertive than me. They are terrific creatures who have pushed through the bollards of chauvinism to take their rightful places on the steps of journalistic history, while also having great hair. Emily Maitlis has a regular home-visiting hairdresser. A former general in the Albanian army zooms round to her house on a motorbike and sorts her hair out every week. Dame Joan laughs openly about not having the faintest idea what colour her hair has been for the last four decades. Nora Ephron wasn't quite as enthusiastic about how much time and effort went into maintaining her hair – a glossy, heavy-fringed, short and sassy affair – but she was adamant that she was not going to go gracefully into the grey-haired good night. She saw how age discrimination affected women more than men and was honest and open about how much that affected her judgement about her own appearance. Greying around the temples is a sign of wisdom and experience in Brian, but it's a sign of being tired and getting on a bit in Barbara.

Don't think for a moment that isn't playing out in my shallow brain, too, although, while we're on the subject of men, I also think that going bald may be something that we, as women, don't fully appreciate. I don't know a woman who gives a monkeys about men losing their hair. I've never, ever heard a friend say they wouldn't date a bald man, or that they have lost interest in their husbands or partners because they are getting a bit thin on top. But I don't think that message really gets through to men, and because we don't think much of it, I suspect that we don't really understand just how strange and frightening it must be to see your hair fall out, to look in the mirror in your thirties or forties and see your appearance changing so much. We laugh quite openly at what men do to their hair, don't we? It's considered fair game to make a news story out of someone who has had a weave put in, or who always wears a cap indoors (while we are here, gentlemen, there is never a time for a jauntily placed kepi unless you are on the stage in a musical, and even then it's annoying). I think we might need to talk a bit more about that. Obviously, we are still allowed to laugh openly at Trump and Giuliani, two buffoons of male-hair idiocy, whose comical coiffuring and horrendous home-dyeing are only matched by the landscape of lunacy going on in their actual brains. They both have the hair they deserve.

Before the final credits roll in this hair saga, obviously I'm going to bung in the caveat that I do *know* we should strike out against this mega-industry of vanity, the one that plays on our sense of what youth and beauty is. The damage young men and women can do to themselves chasing an image that their bodies cannot sustain is horrendous. I know that ever since that tender age of ten a bit of me has always judged myself harshly, and I mean really harshly, in a world that says I am never good enough, attractive enough, or possessed of exactly the right hair.

But if I find a tiny bit of fun in the playground of shampoo and set then I'm going to enjoy every second of that, if you don't mind. Do I understand that there is more to life than having nice hair? Yes, I do. If I was down in the dumps, would I *genuinely* be made happier by the purchase of another hair serum that promised, using only the power of terrible chemicals, to transform the brittle twigs of my hair into sleek, God-like curls? Oh yes, baby, baby I most certainly would.

I am proud to say that hair makes me happy – the vacuous exploration of it, the sheer appointment I have with it every day. Finding a surprising sense of content-ment in my fifth decade might actually have as much to do with landing on a hairstyle and colour that I like as it is to do with the settling of hormones, of family life and the thankful passing of the low-rise jean as a thing. Oh yes, there are hidden shallows to my depths.

And I'm not criticising my kind mum at all from a forty-year distance because she said in the moment what she felt I needed to hear, and it came from a place of love. But what would I tell that chubby ten-year-old, knowing that a glance of self-loathing can corrode tiny lives and send something so dark and festering deep within you that a lifetime of self-doubt might begin? I'd say come on, let's go and celebrate something shiny and bouncy instead! Get your wands! Get your rollers! Get your huge brushes! Let's go and do something really magical with your hair!

JANE

I SHOULD SAY THAT I have heard Fi's hair crack. It has interrupted podcast recordings in the past. I did try to ignore it, as you do with a maiden aunt who's just had a flatulent disturbance when rising to her tiny feet, but even I have some professional standards. Not many, I grant you.

Hair-wise I am currently a full-blooded, fifty-seven-year-old conker with subtle hints of Sheeran and the merest suggestion of grey at the roots. It's thick, and it's wiry. My Pandemic Head has been erased, after a wonderful reunion with the long-suffering staff at 'my' salon. I know it was probably my feminist duty to use the closure of hairdressers to go elegantly grey, and I thought about it. But not for very long. I fell right back into the salon's arms, though obviously not literally, as I've been an enthusiastic social distancer most of my life, long before it was The Law. The whole thing was utter bliss. I have simply never been more eager to hear all about the sleeping arrangements planned for my colourist's much-anticipated villa holiday in Cyprus in August. I was well into my forties before I learned to properly enjoy my quality time at the hairdresser's, sinking into this comfortable world of shared confidences after a sneaky peek at a reality TV star's granite kitchen island, laid bare in the pages of *Hello!*. I have always wondered how they answer the phone there, by the way. Do they say, 'Hello, *Hello!*', which sounds dangerously close to the girls and boys in blue, or do they go for a more formal 'Good Morning, *Hello!*' Please don't ring to check.

I used to dread the hairdresser's when I was a teenager because I had NO appropriate chat. None of what we now know to be 'banter'. Nothing to offer. Zilch. I most emphatically WASN'T going out tonight, no. I would be going home, where I might rearrange my collection of coloured vinyl or write a few lines of poetry. My poor vision (I never wore my glasses in public) was a blessing, because I was spared the sight of my face, except the blurred version that comes at you when you do a hopeful, myopic squint. The poor stylist would try to coax me into some sort of opinion about the style, but I genuinely didn't have one. I just wanted it over with. And that's not an actual style. Although you still see it about.

Back in the 1980s I was never bold enough for 'Sun In' (I think that was for the faster girls – go Fi), but as a diminutive brunette intellectual I was certainly an enthusiastic Shader and Toner. I wouldn't be surprised if there are still hints of warm amber in my tresses to this day. We'll get Forensics on to it, guv.

And the Boots counter. Oh, I've been there. These days I may steam in, head straight for the Epsom Bath Salts and the Vitamin D, snigger at the notion of serum and then buy some and be done with it. But back then the place was as close as we got to a palace of promise. There was no Instagram pummelling you with joyless perfection. It was all about the Boots . . . lingering, gazing longingly at the visions in the ads and on the packaging. Smokey hues. Frosted blues. Beguiling, full, ruby-red lips. Come hither. And do what? No idea. But I've got a brilliant Spandau Ballet twelve-inch back in my room, if you're interested.

Like Fi, I too was beginning the lifelong tussle with my appearance, starting to make simple but necessary improvements, acknowledging my obvious flaws, learning to live with my awkward, imperfect self. You can keep your wit and your brains, and you learn that early on. They're useful; they're just not enough. I knew I was short, for a start. Just as someone who is tall surely knows they are tall, I knew I was short. But if I ever forgot, there was always someone around to remind me. Why, whenever we did graphs in Maths, did we ALWAYS focus on height in the class? Well-meaning old folk would offer up a consolation head-pat and the wisdom that there was 'good stuff in little parcels'. Is there bad stuff in big ones? A friend of the family had laughingly told me I had 'legs like Norman Hunter'. Norman played for Leeds United, gloried in the nickname 'Bite Yer Legs', and was usually associated with the adjective 'stocky'. This was not good news, though. It might have been marginally better if he'd played for Liverpool. I did say marginally. Why do I still remember this? I wish I didn't. But you know you don't forget. I bet everyone reading this has a moment, a memory, a point at which someone – almost always your senior or superior in some way, or someone who did indeed love you very much – sized you up and found you wanting. And had no problem with saying so. Perhaps because they'd already lived your future and hadn't liked it very much. And I should face the fact that I may have been one of those people, too. Oh Lord. What have I said? What seeds have I planted?

3

CATHEDRAL TO SPARE:

PROFESSIONAL SCOUSERS AND
HOMETOWN NOSTALGIA

JANE

I'M FROM LIVERPOOL. Have I ever mentioned it? Yes, because I'm from Liverpool.

The Professional Scouser is an annoying breed. There are plenty of us about, and it's undeniable that an extraordinary number of us have chosen to make our homes some distance away from Liverpool, the place we purport to love so much. The world of show-biz is absolutely awash with Liverpudlian legends, accents all over the shop, an unwavering sentimentality about Merseyside and huge, gated mansions in the deep, deep South of England. They drive golf buggies around Virginia Water and say things like 'I'm quitting Britain if the Tories get in,' but then they don't when they do.

I'm not a golfer (yet), but you can't argue with the plain facts: I was born in Liverpool, in 1964. Which on the Scouse Credentials-Ometer gets me quite a high score. My parents met at the Cavern Club, actually. They spotted each other in the crush as Paul and John rasped out 'Twist and Shout' in one of those legendary lunchtime gigs, sweat coursing down the walls.

Oh, all right then. The first bit is true – I WAS born in the coolest place on earth at the best possible time. But Mum and Dad actually met at a disappointingly respectable sports club in Hightown, a rural stop on the railway line between Liverpool and Southport, the sun-drenched capital of the Mersey Riviera. And neither of them ever went to the Cavern. I'm told it was 'a bit common'. Of course it was.

That simple phrase tells you a great deal about my background. Thumping great tomes are written, epic films are made, but we must never forget all the little people who could have been a small part of history. But weren't, because it was spotting with rain and they didn't fancy it. Because they had a slight problem with their left ankle. Because an iconic music venue was 'a bit common'. Well, ladies and gentlemen, I spring from these people. Never mind. I've always said the Garvey family motto should be 'I wouldn't if I were you.' Or 'Best not.' In fairness, I can say my mum knew someone at the hairdresser's who claimed personal knowledge of Macca, so I have a personal link: my mum might have had a basin hair wash close to a woman who'd had a bit of Beatle.

I really don't mean to be disparaging about places that aren't Liverpool, but there are some parts of Britain that inspire comment or conversation. If you're from Bakewell in Derbyshire you have the lovely tart, and in

Eccles you have the cake (and I'm sure there are other locations not linked directly to puddings and pies), but there are many more about which there is literally nothing to say. For example, you may have been born in Guildford or Dunstable and, if so, I wish you well. No doubt, if you tried hard enough you could lay claim to ownership of a superb one-way system or a notable Victorian poet. But what are the rest of us supposed to say? A good friend once entered a radio poetry competition about birthplaces and won with the epic: 'Surrey. Sorry.' Very moving in its own way.

But it can't be denied, Liverpool's a conversation starter. It gets people talking, and its citizens talk like no one else in the country. The wonderfully expressive word 'gobshite' is defined in Scouse thus: 'someone who speaks too much'. It comes from an Irish expression meaning a 'stupid, foolish or incompetent person'. A lot about Liverpool comes from Ireland, of course, including most of its inhabitants. My dad's traced his family back to a chap called Peter who turned up in Liverpool in 1840 from Armagh, in the north of the country. My paternal grandmother's maiden name was Taylor, so she sounds resolutely English, but that's about it for Englishness in my DNA. The female line is a heady brew of O'Neills and O'Hares. 'Irish royalty!' according to my maternal grandmother, who was certainly very regal. Perhaps that explains why I would often be sent on secret missions ('Don't tell your mother!') to get her liquid paraffin from the chemist. Nanna was a martyr to her digestive system, you see. But then that's the aristocracy for you. Very delicate.

So what do you get, then, when you mix sea air with a big, creamy dollop of Irish charm and some pure, Northern English grit? I'm afraid the answer's all too simple: you get Britain's most defiant, funny and creative people, that's what. And the most inquisitive, too, with my father the exception proving the rule. You could approach him with a limb hanging off, several rings through your nose and an incontinent penguin on your head and he'd probably still greet you with a mild 'Hello there, how was the journey?'

I'm happy to clamber on board the sentimental Scouse-wagon, the maudlin *Northern Express*, busily perpetuating the common myth that we're a very special sort of people.

I always knew that Scouse uniqueness was well worth celebrating. Back in the late 1970s at guide camp, we'd gather around the fire and sing in the evening. How twee that sounds – but I don't care. Mock all you like. We'd dutifully rattle through 'Ten Green Bottles' and maybe 'Kumbaya', and then it was on to the good stuff: a rousing version of 'My Father's a Lavatory Cleaner', followed at day's end by the genuinely stirring 'In My Liverpool Home', originally by the folk group The Spinners. Not a dry eye in sight as the sun went down and we sang with such yearning about our long-lost home city, with its bare statue outside Lewis's department store, the Pier Head the Jerries couldn't destroy, and not one but two cathedrals – Catholic and Protestant, a cathedral to spare. It seemed so distant. An impossible dream. It only dawned on me recently that we were usually camped somewhere in Lancashire, probably less than fifty miles or about an hour away down the M6, given a fair wind.

But that was then. Who am I now to say anything about a place I haven't lived in, properly, since I was eighteen? You could certainly argue that I'm just a female version of the jowly Northern comic with the place in Virginia Water, only I've got a passing acquaintance with *The Mill on the Floss*, and the way I speak tells you almost nothing about who I really am. Or was. Oh, and I'm nowhere near as entertaining as the proper Scouser. But honestly, I think the soft-rock gods The Eagles were right: you can stuff everything in your overnight bag and head down to reception but . . . you know the rest.

Anyway, my parents still live there and, pre-pandemic, I was a regular on the Euston to Liverpool run. Oh, Euston. What a bloody hole. The ultimate monument to 1960s crapism, it will always look like a building assembled in a tearing hurry by someone who couldn't be bothered to read the instructions. There's an undeniable majesty about Paddington. You can almost whiff the Cornish sea air. St Pancras positively oozes Continental possibilities, baguettes and Gauloises. But Euston, low-slung and grey, says glumly, yes, you can get to Runcorn direct from here, if you must. I sometimes think I may have given six months of my life to staring at the Euston Station noticeboard, waiting for the elusive platform confirmation. I'm almost certain they delay the Liverpool announcement, by the way. People travelling to Milton Keynes always seem to get plenty of warning, while we have to sprint for the platform with seconds to spare. Paranoia? No, I just think they're out to get us, those Southern Softy noticeboard tweakers.

Timing is everything in life, so take a tip: avoid the Liverpool train on a Friday afternoon, unless you're totally at ease sharing the carriage with Essex hen parties furiously necking Cava and waving around their anatomically correct inflatables. I've just realised how uncharitable and joyless that sounds. I'm writing this in the grim pandemic winter, and it has occurred to me that, right now, I'd give anything to be staggering grumpily down a packed train with a grab bag of salt and vinegar, getting bopped on the head by a giant penis. Come back, normal life, and bring your inflatable male reproductive organs with you.

Going back is a strange thing. I know, I know: a day trip to Liverpool does not make me Captain Intrepid, or even Michael 'Maverick Trousers' Portillo, but for me it's time travel, dipping into absurdly familiar waters, then lurching back on a slightly whiffy Avanti West to what passes for my reality again.

The time travel feels still more surreal because I can do it all in a day: up early in West London, Tube, train, short walk across the city, Merseyrail to Crosby. Then home again by 9.30 p.m., and always so tired, though I've barely moved a muscle all day. And I do mean 'home' – I know home's not Liverpool any more. But stating it so baldly is still a stupidly difficult thing to do. It feels almost disloyal. The state of HER, who does she think she is? All tofu, and cashmere jumpers and retro occasional tables. Gets her teabags from the World Food aisle! I know that's what I'd think about me. Because I nearly wasn't me. I'm only this version of me because of a letter I wrote in April 1987, which landed on a desk at a radio station in Worcester at just the right time. If I had waited a day . . . or sent it too early . . . I wouldn't be me at all. Every life has moments like this, I know. It's probably better not to indulge those slithery thoughts of *Sliding Doors*.

My Liverpool may not be the Liverpool you think you know, either. Crosby is now best known for the Antony Gormley installation *Another Place*. Its wide, flat beach, with views right across to the snowy peaks of North Wales, is now the permanent home to an army of generously barnacled, naked Iron Men, gazing wistfully at the horizon. Its streets, barely six miles from the city centre, hum gently with middle-class aspiration, not gritty despair. Though anyone who can travel north by road from Lime Street Station to the suburbs and not see real poverty and deprivation along the way, even now, is fooling themselves. At my primary school in Waterloo there was at least one boy in my class who shared shoes with his siblings, so couldn't come in every day. Maybe that doesn't happen anymore. But food banks are well used, and much-needed.

Despite the cliché of the hard-done-by Scouser, I can never claim any personal experience of hardship. My childhood was cushioned and cosy: we lived in an avenue of roomy semis where men called Des spent most of Sunday buffing up their Austin Allegros, and women got on with the gravy. The Freemasons were something of a force, though, to my dad's credit, it wasn't for him: 'What a load of cobblers.' He probably didn't fancy the apron. The Garveys may not be natural risk-takers, but we do come equipped with fully functioning bullshit-detectors. I would claim that as a Scouse trait too, really. Sometimes I entertain myself wondering what long-dead members of my family would make of the modern world. What might my laconic Grandad Jim O'Neill, an enthusiastic regular at the Endbutt public house, have to say about eyebrow-threading or jackfruit or Channel 5+1?

Liverpool is a famously loyal Labour city, but Crosby had a Conservative MP even until 1981, when Shirley Williams (untidy hair, mighty brain) won the seat for the newly formed SDP. Now that event was truly seismic, propelling our dull suburb into the national headlines and making me positively giddy with excitement. Sitting around in the front room (in those days you had no choice but to watch the TV *en famille*, however uncomfortable that was), there was a collective gasp when the great Angela Rippon actually SAID 'Crosby' on the Nine O'clock News. I was seventeen and, finally, here was glorious proof we really did exist. The place was briefly overrun by members of the press and film crews, all of whom seemed arrogant, urgent and overbearing. I became even more determined to pursue this line of work in later life.

Earlier that year, weeks before the royal wedding of Charles and Diana, the Toxteth riots in inner-city Liverpool had dominated the headlines for days. To my shame, I honestly had no real idea where Toxteth was, nor what its problems were. My trips into 'town' were restricted to the clothes shops on Church Street, just getting on with the terrible stuff of teenage life and loathing what I saw in the always unforgiving changing-room mirrors in Chelsea Girl.

On 6 July 1981 I record in my diary: 'So far 250 policemen have been injured . . . this is England and this, unfortunately, is Liverpool. To think I have to include "Liverpool" in my address . . .' I thunder, like someone about to attend her first Conservative Party conference and make a fiery and ill-judged speech from the podium in a very high voice. I then move seamlessly on to give a breathless account of the complicated internal politics of the Merchant Taylors' Joint Schools' Debating Society. Or 'Deb Soc'. You can draw your own conclusions here. If it helps, I also describe the royal wedding as 'incredibly romantic'.

My ignorance is as good as any of my relative privilege. And, yes, much else besides. My parents were clerical workers (Mum at the hospital, Dad at the Dock

Board) and we holidayed in slightly damp seaside chalets in North Wales; not luxury properties in St Lucia but, nevertheless, I may as well have been on another planet from rioters in Toxteth.

At school, we'd all been heavily influenced by ITV's lavish adaptation of Evelyn Waugh's *Brideshead Revisited* and one or two of the lads we knocked about with had even, daringly, experimented with cravats. Believe me, it took raw courage to ape the fey, flailing aristo Sebastian Flyte on Merseyside public transport in the early 1980s, so fair play. I don't think any of them took it as far as carting a teddy about, mind you.

I think it may have been one of the plucky cravat wearers who would memorise *Monty Python* sketches, and then seek to transfix the fairer sex at parties. And when I say transfix, I mean I at least would be bored rigid. I think it was the first time I realised I was expected to be in the audience while a 'chap' performed. It was apparently my job to giggle and swoon a bit, and I already knew this was going to be a lifelong challenge. Even now, I'm in awe of those women who are happy to giggle on cue and can pull all the right faces, even if they've heard the bloody story a thousand times before. I learned then to dive head-first into the Snowballs and cherry brandy. Swooning was certainly a lot easier when you were a few Snowballs to the good.

The sad truth is that most of that teenage crowd of mine left Merseyside for university in the early 1980s and simply never went back, at least not to live. Liverpool at that time was not exactly a land of opportunity, and our parents had encouraged us to be ambitious. Perhaps, though, they hadn't realised that ambition would mean we had to leave, probably for good.

And so we're exiles, in some cases professional ones. Proud of our roots and sometimes still trading on them. I know I certainly carry my Scouse belligerence with me, however familiar I may now be with West London's idiosyncrasies. I'll have a flat white please. Oat. Three quid? Blimey. Anyway, it probably wasn't a great idea of mine to refer to some BBC management figures as 'tinpot tyrants in chinos', in retrospect. Though I'm still quite proud of the phrase, which is why I'm shamelessly repeating it here. And some of them are.

I can still recall the occasion years ago when a pompous member of the London Parks Constabulary, who happened to be bald, admonished me for my inadequate buggy technique at a zebra crossing as he drove along in his van. Before I knew it I'd bawled, 'Oh keep your bloody hair on, Inspector Morse!' to the alarm of my buggied toddler, who'd only really known me as a rather benign, soothing presence. It's telling that I can remember this incident and clearly hold it close to my bosom, so perhaps my wonderful Scouse wit isn't deployed as frequently as I might imagine. And I'm not saying someone from Tunbridge Wells wouldn't have reacted so swiftly.

Or am I?

FI

I THINK YOU PROBABLY ARE.

Gosh, gosh – identity. I'm never sure how to respond to that one. I'm not terribly fond of the question 'Where are you from, but where are you *really* from?' Hasn't it proved to be one of the most dangerous of our times? Wherever you ask it, or whomever you aim it at, it can so easily weaponise what is the sheer lottery of where you tumbled out into the world. It's usually about confirming a stereotype, sealing someone in their past, making it easier for the asker to believe they already know the story without really knowing much about an individual life. And of course there isn't any serious collateral damage caused to people like you and me in talking about family identity, what on earth would we know about the prejudice that corrodes a life, damages an opportunity and steals away a chance before it can be taken. But it's a funny one isn't it, because maybe just by still celebrating the benevolent stereotypes, you keep a place on the shelf for the less fortunate ones – and in doing that you simply keep prejudice alive.

In this instance you might also be thinking that response may well be considered and nuanced, and taking it all too seriously, too, when perhaps I am just having a fit of pique because I can't bring to the table such a cultural plethora of good fortune. I was born in Slough. I didn't realise I had to say 'Slough: sorry'. Then raised in

Hampshire, near Basingstoke, then Winchester. I know, Jane, that you like to envisage 'The South' as some kind of weird mash-up of *Howard's Way* and *Howard's End* and Michael Howard's constituency. Basically, people being nasty to each other, possibly on yachts, many of them called Howard. I'd defend it to the hilt but, apart from driving through Hampshire on the way to somewhere else, I've not really been back since I was seventeen. The county's cultural claim to fame would have to be Jane Austen, who lived near Alton, but even she headed off whenever she could, stocking up with a family sized bag of Wotsits and a big bottle of Diet Coke to see her through the vagaries of the A303 on her way to Bath, to witness all of those Regency antics in the less bachelor deprived county of Wiltshire.

If you want to really overindulge in that kind of drawing room caricature then you'll assume that most of us 'from The South' are rarely out of a marquee – you earthy Scousers probably imagine everyone to be in there celebrating Robert's wonderful union with Venetia, competing over who bought the best set of fish knives for them on their wedding list and wondering how soon we can get back to feed the labradors. In this stereotype the thing we most dread, more than someone cutting the Stilton the wrong way or getting a spillage on the cashmere cardi, is getting stuck next to someone from Liverpool with their non-stop one-way 'dialogue' about how remarkable/fascinating/culturally significant/ important etc. the city is. Even a quick 'Is Derek Hatton still with us?' can rarely stem the Mersey flow. How can we possibly compete? And yes, you do appear to have made this into a competition.

I suppose that, as you so astutely point out, at least the marquee is now full of non-Southerners due to the undoubted appeal of the golf courses and the warm welcome that everyone has learned from having to share the green with 'new people'. Instead of incomers being met with a surly 'You're not from round here, are you?' they're more likely to get an astonished 'You *are* from around here?' if it turns out they have any remote connection to the area. You are right that whole swathes of Surrey have been mercilessly infiltrated with people from your neck of the woods. It's as if they feel at home there.

Go anywhere else in the world and explain to people the divide between the North and South of England and they'll be puzzled by the sheer notion that there even is a North and South of a country that is so small by comparison to most. It takes longer to get from one side of Mumbai to the other, or Mexico City or any of the Chinese supercities, than it does to get from where I was born (Slough) to where you were born (Crosby), so what are we slicing and dicing about?

And is home still where you came from? Or is it where you settle?

I suddenly feel a strong urge to defend all the people who came from a small place that was near a bigger place that had no huge cultural significance. And then they moved anyway. Perhaps that is exactly who I am.

I think my dad once lived in a house that was next to a house that once had some of Fleetwood Mac staying in it. Will that impress you at all? Damn. You win.

I have at times had to take the train out of Waterloo, Paddington and King's Cross to go and see my mum, but for most of my childhood and early adulthood it wasn't a London train station I had to get to – it was Terminal 3 at about five in the morning and the start of a long journey out to Hong Kong to see my dad, who had left to go and work there in 1974. Back then it was a long flight of twenty-four hours and three or four stopovers. Paris, Athens, Tehran, Kuwait, Bangkok, Delhi. I stand more chance of finding affinity with someone who knows the way through the In Transit system of Dubai Airport as you do with someone who can key into the early classics of Gerry and the Pacemakers.

But affinity is a very useful thing for lots of us; if you don't have a huge thing to look back on – the anchor of a cultural identity – you have to set your own path.

Like so many people I've come to depend on it. It's there in a shared reaction to the tiniest thing with a stranger, it's in a passing reference to a person or a song or a story, it's the feeling that you know a place even when you have only just arrived.

I found a bit of an affinity in Dalston – the bit of East London that lurks with no real identity between Islington and Hackney.

I have lived happily in E8 for twenty-three years now. It's where my kids were born. Hopefully it will be where they can say they're from. I had absolutely no known connection to Dalston before I came to look at a one up, one down railwayman's cottage here years ago. These terraced houses were built for the men who worked on the railway line that snakes out of London to the big skies of Suffolk and the bustling towns of Essex, and I just liked it here as soon as I arrived.

And there was a spooky coincidence. My Granny Grace (Mum's mum) was by that time in her late nineties, in a care home in Oxford, and I'd go and see her for tea on a Sunday, not often enough mind you. You got liquid paraffin for yours, I preferred to take a bunch of flowers for mine. And one weekend I took the details of the house with me to show her. She handed them straight back to me, clearly upset. It took a while for her to tell me that the house was just a couple of streets away from where some of her family had lived and worked years before. One of her uncles had run a horse-drawn carrier's business. Some aunts were housekeepers or companions, two of them seamstresses employed by the local convent. They didn't seem to be easy memories to share so I didn't ask any more questions, even though I had at least 234 ready to go.

Because her life was intriguing. Grace left school at fourteen. She was really bright, and particularly good at maths. A promising job as a bookkeeper was cut short when that all too familiar long arm of caring responsibility reached out into her young adult life and called her home. Her father asked her to come back and look after her mother, who had been diagnosed with cancer – and whom she nursed till she died when Grace was only eighteen. It's no surprise some memories were difficult. But during that time when she cared for her Mum the local GP had spotted her bright mind and empathetic talents and encouraged her to train as a nurse, which she did with dedication at UCH in London.

And there she met my grandfather – a young surgeon called Chassar Moir. He was a long way from home. His family ran the grocer's shop, William Moir and Sons, on the High Street in Montrose, a pretty but chilly town (don't say I didn't warn you) high up on the east coast of Scotland. He was brainy, too. That brain powered him through the local academy and on to university in Edinburgh. He became a doctor, which took him to London and UCH, and from there he became a professor, specialising in obstetrics and gynaecology – and here's our family's greatest achievement and why I'm telling you, because it defines our clan so much more than place or class or whatever you want to look for in order to believe you know the story of a person. Chassar researched and developed the drug ergometrine, which stops you and me and millions of women all over the world from haemorrhaging during labour. His quiet work saved countless lives. He was a modest man, too (not all family traits have been passed down), seeking no patent or massive pats on the back. And his work changed the direction of the family. He never went back to live in Montrose. Grace had to give up her nursing career when she got married – those were the rules back then. They had four children; his work took him all over the world but they raised their family in Oxford. Chassar died at the age of seventy-seven. Granny Grace died when she was ninety-seven. We never really spoke of Dalston again.

So maybe that was my affinity. A strange feeling that Dalston and me did have a connection. Or – and I think we might agree that this is more likely – perhaps it's just that people who move around a bit do in fact need to find a soft piece of ground into which to bang their posts. We cling to the tiniest of pulls, we need to be ready with something when someone asks the inevitable 'where are you from?' question.

Anyway, back to you. I suspect that I do envy you having such firm roots. I can't imagine how comforting that must often be, but is it also just a tiny bit limiting sometimes? Wouldn't you be the funny, sharp wisecracking lady you are today wherever you had been born? I know that Liverpool is tremendous, really I do. You've told me often enough. But don't let it take credit for too much. You moved away and made something totally your own. The Mersey beat isn't the only rhythm of your life.

And yes, bloody Euston. You are so very right about that passenger information board. I like to imagine that it's run from a viewing deck somewhere and that any member of staff who's had to put up with offensive, rude, drunk or inflatable penis people is allowed to go there for a special treat at the end of their shift when they play 'RUN FOR YOUR MERSEY LIFE!', a unique game where you do indeed wait until the concourse is so crowded that people can barely move – and then . . . tickertickerticker . . . wait for it . . . yup! The 17.14 does usually go from platform 2 – but yo, suckers! TODAY IT'S PLATFORM 15! RUN! EVERYBODY, RUN!

4

STEAM-CLEAN MY GWYNETH!:

SELF-IMPROVEMENT AND ORGASM MERCH

FI

SHOULD WE ALL PUT OUR orgasms up on Pinterest, Jane? Should they form part of our 'story?'. Perhaps we could workshop them. I could tell you how yours could be better with no other qualification than my own personal experience. By the very nature of that word 'personal' it is impossible for you to know whether or not my advice is good. Simply because I'm telling you that mine are terrific, I'm making you feel that maybe yours aren't. I'm thinking about starting an online forum, calling it a 'community' but, make no mistake, I'm the one in charge of it all. When that becomes successful maybe I'll be able to turn it into a brand. My favourite name choice so far is MoreGasms. *Curtseys.*

Pretty soon, with my business plan of daft (which is accompanied by my spreadsheet of delusion), I'll have made a leap to merchandising. And it's the merch that makes you rich. Within a couple of years my 'start-up' – never just a company, always a 'start-up' – could be flogging matching cashmere loungewear. You'll be able to buy my branded jogging bottoms for £367. You might think I am exaggerating with that price tag but I'm really not. There's always something for £367 on a twit's website. Maybe 367 is the series of numbers identified by the numerologist who came in to 'numberise' More-Gasms' new offices in Shoreditch, housed in a block called White Collar Factory. Isn't that a clever, ironic name – like, a whole factory for people who have never been in a factory?

Well actually the factory is where fiction meets fact. White Collar Factory is real. Only it's not just an office block, it's an 'urban campus' on Old Street roundabout in the heart of London's answer to Silicon Valley. 'Urban campus' is how the people who built the building de-scribe it, not me. You can't just have an office block any more. You have to tinker with the way you describe everything. Raise the game. Recalibrate it. Optimise it. I bet they've gone beyond the ubiquitous 'breakout area' in there, maybe full circle to some kind of ironic sign that simply says 'Meeting Room 1'. Oh how we laughed. It's where the actual factories of Shoreditch used to be, back in the day, when the area churned out furniture and fabrics and matches – when people only had time and energy to concentrate on things they needed.

Although, of course, that's not entirely true. It's always been part of the human condition to want to stretch towards something 'other' – be that religion, spirituality or enhanced sensory pleasure. It's taken mankind on a journey (have I really just said that?) from studying the entrails of animals in Ancient Greece, to the reading of palms, to third-eye therapy, to 'tapping into your seven chakras' on a beach in Ibiza. We're drawn to anything that can promise us a truth we think we can't quite reach ourselves.

I get a lot of offers at the moment to 'reconnect with myself'. Strangely, this is always someone else offering to do the reconnection for a not inconsiderable fee. A holiday company this week invited me to Greece to 'activate my inner powers' at a series of beach-based workshops, and a leaflet that came through the letterbox yesterday asked me if I wanted to stay home in Dalston and 'tap into the intuitive you' with an online course in Tarot card-reading. The leaflet had some typos and spelling mistakes and the intuitive me is saying, if you can't spell repetitive ('Are you having repetative negative thoughts?') then you may not have my money.

There's nothing wrong with needing that extra affirmation – or attention – or just moments of zing in life. It's a confusing world out there, especially at the moment. And I'm grateful for what I've got. I am not existing below the poverty line, my health is fine. For now. I have a vote. Rights. I can afford a weekly shop to feed me and my children and the bills get paid. This is all we should hope to have in life, isn't it? But there is still a near-constant buzz, one that is getting louder and louder, going, 'It's still not quite enough, still not enough'?

Who cares? you might ask. If you are in a world where you have the basics, then lucky you, what does it matter to anyone else that people, or aggressive algorithms, see you as a sucker with a loose wallet and some menopausal anxiety to play with? You might argue that the world of the gong bath, the prophetic crystals and the cashmere 'laccy pants' (as the elasticated-waist trouser is known in our household) is only being milked at the top of the privilege mountain, BUT the influence – and appeal of commercialising it all – is very real. Once you've got a whole shelf of votive candles at your local supermarket and the laundromat is reopening as a flotation tank parlour, and even your socks claim to have vitamins in them, you know that the trickle-down effect is working. It *does* matter that dissatisfaction is being sold so well. The mantra of the West Coast elite – the notion that to be alive is not enough, you must thrive, too – has very much joined our collective psyche.

Apart from what that ethos does to our own levels of contentment and self-esteem, it also leaves us no longer knowing how to judge anyone else's success or happiness. It's an endless comparison where the bar gets higher and higher. Do you look well, or are you radiant? Is your hair still there or is it *luxuriant*? Are you content with your man/woman/single status/whomever you choose? Well, content is not enough, you must now be fulfilled. And would you mind sharing that sense of fulfilment in a public way please, otherwise you're making the rest of us feel uncomfortable with your privacy? God forbid anyone would have the stench of anonymity around them in these modern times.

If I sound cynical and shouty, that is because I am. I am also a hypocrite.

I know these things because I have answered the call of the muppetry. Two summers ago I went to what billed itself as a 'medical spa'. I saved my pennies and needed to; I could have bought a small second-hand car for the same price. The trip was more about needing to go somewhere where I wouldn't feel odd being on my own and sad seeing other families at play as it was about wanting to indulge in the many and varied treatments on offer. I wanted to be given a legitimate reason to lie down in a dark room in the daytime. It allowed me to do all those things. And so much more. And I'd got it very, very wrong.

It was very, very 'inner self'-driven. All about the 'me'. All about 'resetting'. They actually called it a 'cure', although they never stipulated what it was you were being cured of. There was an oxygen bank where you could pay to sit and breathe air. There were coconut mouthwashes for you to swill away the 'bad bacteria' in your mouth. You could have special German leeches flown in to suck out your 'bad blood'. Colonic irrigation – the original bedfellow of the digestively challenged – was available, too. On Thursdays you could have a curse placed on you, only to have it lifted to release your inner spirit on Friday. I am making that up, but you probably believed me and that's the point. You were meant to eat in silence. 'Monotony' was advocated. There was absolutely no normal bread.

Food is so problematic in the world of thriving. Take bread. Oh please just take some bloody bread will you? Bread is not the enemy, people. A sensitivity is not an allergy, and please don't wish a proper allergy on yourself. Food exclusion seems to be the starting point of a very expensive journey to a nirvana that is often called something wafty like a 'cure' or a 'reset' or an 'activation'. I'm nervous about anyone who is selling a form of denial, unless they are also promising to be there with you when your self-control trips the switch, and the replenishing of that denial sweeps over you.

Back at the spa there were 'salts' you were meant to take every day to 'cleanse your intestines'. Basically they gave you very expensive diarrhoea. I opted not to take them. Everybody else did, which meant you'd be halfway through a chat with a fellow inmate over a cup of acrid cleansing tea when a lurchy kind of expression would come across their face and they'd have to rush off. It seemed ever so undignified. At lunch and dinner we ate tiny portions. We were given tiny spoons. You weren't meant to drink water with your meal for some odd reason. And so the rules went on. It was a form of imposed unpleasantness delivered in a pseudo-sciency way to a group of people who should be smart enough to know better. Before leaving (four days early, enough was enough) I went back to the person in a white coat who might have been a doctor, but who really knows, and she congratulated me on doing so well on 'the cure' – blood pressure down, weight trimmed, better skin. I didn't have the balls to say I'd not actually done the cure. Those benefits had come from simply not being in the hurly-burly of my normal life. Silly sausage. That's me, not her.

I know, I know. A fool and her money are easily parted. I apologise to the universe for my fallibility.

If I could have been more honest with myself, what I needed then was just support. Kind, sincere, nurturing, anonymous support. I think it's what most of us want but it's got confused with a message about being stronger, leaner, better, thinner. A message that everything you need can be found within yourself, at a price, usually sold by people who can't find it themselves either.

And another thing while we're here. What goes up has to come down.

For every hour spent in rhapsody on the reiki couch or at the oxygen bar, there are a considerable number more hours of life to just plod through, attempting an even keel and no more than that. Far from finding your inner balance, much of this self-improvement stuff risks making you very uneven. How are you meant to return to the simple tea-and-biscuit structure of the normal modern world after reaching nirvana? It's easy to crunch through the gears when you're accelerating, that's where you feel the force. It's so much harder to work out the gears on the way down. Where is the end point in a journey of self-discovery? Who signs you off? Where is the class where you are told 'Enough. You're fine as you are.' I bet that one would be packed.

There's another form of self-optimisation I'd like to stop before it really starts.

Let's get to Gwyneth Paltrow and sex. You knew we would, didn't you? Your intuitive self was probably ahead of you there. The multi-award-winning actress and uber-businesswoman is CEO of lifestyle empire Goop – current value £191 million. She's charismatic and beautiful and whip-smart on the old interview repartee. I grudgingly admire her for being able to see, and seemingly embrace, the fact that she is low-hanging fruit for almost-writes-itself copy. Aside from the mind-boggling money, it's just her, isn't it? Her skin is perfect, 'nourished', and so very, very thick. She even says, helpfully, that she doesn't mind if cynical people like me take the mickey out of her empire because it's all clicks to her – GP is from the 'any publicity is good publicity' school of thought. Her slogan 'we're only here once so why not milk the shit out of it' appeals to people whose parents had a copy of Ayn Rand's *The Virtue of Selfishness* on their shelves in the late 1970s.

Gwyneth has nailed it in terms of the inner/outer combo. Although much of her website sells wildly expensive culottes and near-endless recipes featuring salmon and avocado, the stuff that defines Goop is all about the inner self, and most recently there seems to be a lot about sex, seen from a modern female perspective. Gwyneth's photoshoot for the launch of *The Goop Lab* – her TV doc series – had her in front of a massive vagina sculpture made entirely from roses. Perhaps it's a natural progression. Once you have done with the obvious areas of insecurity – how do I look, how do I feel, how do I seem to you – what are you left with? Well, sex obviously. They've come after your face, your hair, your weight, your gut – now they're after your private parts.

Let's rush through the headlines. There are the jade balls that you can wear internally (most doctors say please don't) to 'harness the power of energy work and crystal healing'. There's the now-infamous Mugwort Vagina Steaming Session – Goop advocated this Californian spa therapy where you clean away bad bacteria by sitting on a steamy commode. Again the doctors said no, it's unnecessary and dangerous. Vulva workshop instead, anyone? And then there are the candles, 'This Candle Smells Like My Vagina', retailing at £69, which was followed up with 'This Candle Smells Like My Orgasm'. I bet there are more in the same vein, aren't there? Literally – wax works.

And this is the bit that I can't just dismiss as benign bollocks for people with too much money. I'd like to say, as a thoroughly independent, empowered modern woman, that I really don't know whether the commercial outing of our female organs *is* such a terrific thing. I know I'm meant to say, 'Whooaaaah – way to go, women of the modern world! What a time to be alive!' But I don't want to. Like the sheer notion of MoreGasms, it leaves me feeling a bit queasy.

I don't mean we shouldn't talk about sex. Far from it. And I don't mean we shouldn't enjoy sex either. We absolutely should. Sex education – with a message that its enjoyment is for women, not just men – has never been more vital and necessary in a world where misogynistic imagery is so easy to access and so powerful to see. Let's not be squeamish about it. Our generation, and all those before us, went desperately underprepared into an adult world of sex. Who wouldn't be glad this has changed?

I'm impressed with the level of sex education on the national curriculum alone. It allows me to talk with my kids about what it all means, especially the relationships surrounding sex, in a way that simply never happened in my own childhood. And yes, they find that excruciating, but at least they have the TV gift of *Sex Education* on Netflix, which is divinely honest and funny and kind about something that had none of those attributes back in my own teenage abyss. There was so little said about what might lie outside the sex-to-have-babies discipline that it was hard to imagine there was a place of confidence, let alone difference. Our knowledge and understanding were so limited; our ways of finding out about sex just sad, but comical. A couple of stolen magazines and one dreadful febrile but sterile talk at school was really about it. We clung to whatever knowledge we thought we had got. The rest was just rumour, like the one about how planting pampas grass outside a house meant there were swingers inside. There were a few plumes à Las Pampas outside a couple of bungalows up on the road past school, so for a couple of months we'd cycle past endlessly around 9 p.m. on Saturday in the hope of seeing something going on. If they were swinging, they were doing it quite quietly while watching *The Generation Game*.

There was nothing halcyon about those times. A lack of confidence and female empowerment left us as young women dreadfully vulnerable. Those times were hardly free of porn or the sexual exploitation of women, and men – far from it.

But neither are these current times. The statistics don't show us a world where we as women are remotely close to safe yet. So I think we've gone to the candles too soon. I'm picking on the candles, but you know what I mean – the larger industry of wearing your sexual self on the outside. How the Goopers see themselves – as women rich enough to buy a £69 candle, confident enough to laugh about it, unthreatened by men enough to actually light it in public – well, that might not be how others see them at all.

I'm pretty sure that for every woman who feels empowered by a public mention of their private parts, there is a man who hasn't got the memo. Of course, he should have got it, read it, nudged his brain along and recalibrated how he sees women. It's not every woman's duty to educate every man. But isn't it a simple fact that we haven't got to that place yet? There's still way too much work to be done on the basics before I'd feel comfortable clanking around with the jade ball brigade.

I'm not kowtowing to the male mind or gaze here or telling anyone to be ashamed of their sexuality or curb their libido, if that is what you are shouting at me by now. My end goal of sexual equality for all is hopefully the same as yours. But I also hope we might be a big enough squad, the relatively empowered women squad, to hold different views and shake them around a bit. And maybe could we not forget that we might lie at the top of the pile? So it's important what we say and do, and what we ask for. I am just asking the Goopers to make as much noise about the basic things that are still so stacked against so many women before they turn their not inconsiderable power and influence to making the room smell nice. There's an element of the £69 candles that suggests we're so safe we can all have a laugh about sex. Can we? The real shit is still so bad – rising levels of sexual violence across the world, rape as a weapon of war, men feeling entitled to letch and grope and so much worse – women just feeling that we can't be women without being sexualised. Until that real shit is sorted, is it so very wrong to be a modern woman but want to stay quiet and private about sex?

And I leave you with this thought. Get the gong bath and the Himalayan salt scrub ready, because you'll want to get this out of your mind just as soon as you can. Whenever the pendulum of equality swings out to a new and daring trajectory, it is worth thinking about where that would be on the male equivalent if it swung back – and even in 1974 I don't think anyone really wanted to light a jar called 'This Candle Smells Like My Penis'.

JANE

HARD TO FOLLOW THAT PAY-OFF, but I'll have a go. Let's say it is indeed 1974, a time when men were moustachioed love gods and women just fell at their feet. After a classic 1970s supper of well-cooked gammon with a pineapple ring on top, he'd fire up 'This Candle Smells Like My Penis' (mind you, some men can be a tad sensitive about this sort of thing , so I think it would have sold better if it was called 'This Candle Smells Like MY Penis'), she'd fall quivering into his arms, and they'd get down to it on the shagpile to the raunchy sound of one of the year's biggest hits, 'Remember You're A Womble'.

I must admit, I've been guilty of making Gwyneth and her Goop the punchline of many an easy joke. I hadn't realised the financial extent to which she was very much having the last laugh. £191 million, you say. That's a lot of jade balls. (Insert appropriate health and safety advice here, not the bloody balls, I beg of you.)

If you're rich, white and well connected you may indeed feel free to show your sexual self to the world – though, as Fi says, you still don't have any control over what the world makes of it. You're not safe – just safer.

Still, here is evidence you can indeed build a substantial empire on fluff. Of course, it does depend who's spouting it – I was briefly in the presence of La Paltrow for an interview some years ago and her beauty was of the unnerving, ethereal sort. A genetic wonder of the film world. As a mere mortal, you search these types in vain for any sort of flaw to start with, and then you give up searching and try to drink it all in. Yes, reader, I too would take health and beauty advice from Gwyneth. No, she wasn't eating a Cinnamon Swirl. Imagine if she'd entered the room, wiping her mouth with the back of her hand, telltale pastry flakes on her lips. It never happened, no.

Now were I to initiate a start-up flogging my recommended diet of spicy peanuts, a particular make of no-alcohol lager and a 'lifestyle' brand of roomy, short-leg tracksuit bottoms, I doubt there'd be many takers. Mind you, buying my gear would be a lot cheaper than a stay at Fi's facility (by the way, Mrs, write the screenplay). I think she's probably cured herself of a desire to be made a complete mug of, if nothing else.

I feel quite emotional at the thought of Fi in her room on her last morning at the medical spa, determinedly stuffing her things in a bag and heading down to reception. I admire the fact that she made a plucky bolt for freedom before The End. Whatever that consisted of – what did the survivors get? Was there a 'do' on the last night – a chance to throw caution to the omnipresent wind by chewing your black bread just forty-nine times? Did the most productive colonic irrigator get a couple of extra sachets of trots-inducing tea to enjoy in the comfort of their own home?

It's so frustrating that the people who could really teach us how to live our lives better, who genuinely have wisdom to impart, are the people least likely ever to consider doing such a thing. We are left muddling through with the assistance of an assorted bunch of cranks, professional attention seekers and the people in white coats.

While the West Coast elites may well be meddling with our minds and tying us up in lucrative knots of dissatisfaction, let's not forget that in Silicon Valley the search for eternal life is well under way. The tech kings have long since cracked the orgasm thing, but that was never going to be enough, and they're moving on to great acrobatic sex for all eternity. And before you start thinking there probably are imaginative ways with a Zimmer frame if you really put your mind to it, that's not what they mean. In their future, we will all remain perpetually supple and lusty, forever up-for-it. Yes, even the lactose-intolerant, the gluten-free and the balloon-phobic. I bet Fi can hear the buzz already.

5

WELCOME TO THE PROGRAMME:

BROADCASTING AND GARVEY'S RADIO PERSONALITY ASSESSMENT CHART

JANE

BROADCASTERS AREN'T NORMAL, I'M AFRAID. Jumped-up town criers with knobs on, we're often overwrought and very needy, more to be pitied than admired.

We need a thick skin, but of course we don't have one, or we wouldn't be here in the first place. Broadcasting is where the already insecure huddle together for warmth, and soon find themselves so much more insecure than they could ever have imagined. Tell me I did well and I blush; tell me the programme stank and I blanch. And question your judgement.

I was sent to a life coach by the BBC (I know – that's your licence fee, and there were not inexpensive biscuits), and during the first of six helpful sessions in her cosy sitting room, she quite reasonably asked why I wanted to be a radio presenter. I was momentarily dumbstruck. Surely everyone wanted to do this! I'd always wanted to, certainly. Oh, I know, I'd once thrown inquisitive adults off the scent with some solemn baloney about a career in medicine, but that was just because I knew that was a respectable – if in my case entirely unachievable – ambition. There may be doctors armed only with an O-Level in Biology grade C, but I wouldn't trust them with complex ailments.

For years of my youth, I'd been barfing nonsense into cassette recorders, then there was a wonderful English class when I'd drawn warm applause after performing a radio show from the stationery cupboard, and before that I just enjoyed talking to myself. Still do. It's liberating, and I'm a very good audience. Honestly, if civilisation were to crumble, I'd be only too happy to carry on for as long as possible, addressing the masses through a loudhailer on top of the rubble.

It was 1987. I'd just got the sack from my first 'real' job, as Britain's worst ever advertising account executive. At Hilton Park Services on the M6, over tea and biscuits, I knew I had nothing left to lose. I had to come clean. I told my parents something no one ever needs to hear.

'I just really, really want to be a DJ.'

Of course you do, dear.

Broadcasting is such a brazen thing to do, when you really think about it. To invite yourself into someone else's life and start talking to them. As though you were their real friend, or you knew better than them. How dare we?

I don't think our motivation is hard to find, really: we want, and we like, attention. It's as simple, and as complicated, as that. Under intense questioning, my mother did admit she may have turned up the volume on the *Jimmy Young Show* once or twice to drown out my incessant, colicky wailing. Now I'm neither psychologist nor detective, but you can see what may have happened there. (So look out, young mums, if you're tempted to whack up Clara Amfo to the max when baby's throwing a wobbler.)

Not all broadcasters are monstrous all the time. Though some are, or they're allowed to be. Who knew? Oh darling, everybody knew! Explanations are offered; excuses are given. They're old, they're young, they're tired; they're having a hard time; they're really, really talented. Such a burden, all that talent. And it needs protecting. I have often wondered who benefits from this protection. Do ordinary mortals secretly enjoy working with these demonic legends? Do they hold court in their local, delighting everyone with tales of their star turn's latest crazed demands? And while we're here, does paying for the booze at the Christmas party make up for the fact that you may have been a curmudgeonly arsehole for the rest of the year? It doesn't? Damn.

I should emphasise that I'm talking about the latte-dependent, tantrumming end of the spectrum here – not the utterly horrific. Although as I've got the chance, it cannot be said often enough that the odious Jimmy Savile was also a truly terrible radio presenter. For what it's worth.

Thankfully, most of us are relatively benign figures. Mood swings are an inevitability, apparently, because the stakes are just so high. OK, it's not open-heart surgery, exactly, but no one wants to crash a vocal on a thunderous 1970s disco classic, or make a hash of a pluggy encounter with a renowned thespian staging a comeback. (My personal favourite: 'What first attracted you to the part?' One day a real trouper will say, 'I was out of work and bloody desperate, love.')

Oh, the foibles! Some broadcasters get attached to routine – same train, same pen, those special Big Day pants; their cereal eaten in exactly the same way, from the same bowl, always ending on a sultana. Then there are the bits of studio kit we believe we can't function without. 'Our' chair. The 'right' headphones. For the best part of a decade on *Woman's Hour*, I had to have a decrepit Anglepoise lamp on the studio table, gaffer tape and all. Why? No idea. It barely functioned as a lamp. But I'll tell you something – that was MY old, useless lamp.

If something goes wrong, it's very unlikely to be our fault. If it's a success, then we – naturally – claim all the prizes. There's the classic: 'I'd just like to thank . . .' But we know, deep down, that we could have done this all on our own. Bless the other folk for showing up, though. Aren't they marvellous?

Of course, broadcasting, like any other area of what I'm afraid we must call showbusiness, does have degrees of diabolical. Let me run through some classic personality types for you:

Down to Earth – usually say hello if they see you. (They don't always see you.)

Very Nice – not very successful. Or not as successful as you.

A Real Innovator – had an idea once. Possibly even their own.

Maverick – slippery slope.

National Treasure – for God's sake take the hint and retire, I beg of you!

Larger than Life – call the police. Immediately.

It's very hierarchical, too. At the top of the heap we have the Lite Ent regulars. They're ratings gold, genuine stars, and likely to be bothered by the paps as they 'enjoy lunch in town' or walk their dog to the dry cleaner's in expensive athleisure gear and shades, clutching the now-ubiquitous hot beverage. These ever-smiling folk have crawled over grannies – and that will include their own – to reach the summit of all Celebritydom. Which they soon discover is a lonely, unforgiving and privacy-free space. They then take to drink'n'drugs to cope with it all, and we tut our despair as they flaunt their curves. Then we try to remember to tweet supportively about press intrusion.

In radioland, it's quite simple: your ranking will be determined by the radio hours you occupy. If you're a presenter on a breakfast show, then you're barking-mad, bone-achingly weary but indisputably important. I have some experience in this area, and I can tell you that no one ever forgets their 3.35 a.m. alarm years. Or ever fully recovers. Falling asleep in the afternoon in winter, waking up with a start, drool on the pillow, not knowing whether it's still somehow late today, or possibly tomorrow morning. You're perpetually hollow-eyed, plucky in the face of a number of unglamorous digestive issues, and sick to death of telling people yes, oddly enough, you DO have to get up early. Worth it, though! Think. Of. The. Ratings.

Drive-time hosts are next in the pecking order. Better complexions (more sleep) but chippy, because they're not on Breakfast. Yet. They could do it so much better, you see, SO MUCH better. Whom do they tell? Everyone, usually. Except the presenter currently doing Breakfast, who's actually a really good mate. Apparently.

Now if you're on around lunchtime, that's lovely but . . . you're a mere companion to the overstuffed and often tasteless baguette. Face it. Afternoons? Well, that used to be the place they dumped the token radio Ladies, until they got all these wild ideas about womenfolk with their hormones and high-pitched voices all over the schedules. And if you host a specialist music show in the evening, I'm telling you now that people make jokes behind your back about your dandruff. And that stupid leather jacket.

Radio is still the senior service. The Royal Navy of broadcasting. But let's be honest – there's more money, and more glory, in telly. So, in plain English, you might say – and people do – that radio's for those of us whose appearance doesn't lend itself well to the exacting demands of high-definition television. In even plainer English, it's for far less attractive egomaniacs.

I suppose I should say, in the interests of transparency you understand, that I did very briefly 'go into' television. In its infinite wisdom, the BBC decided what daytime telly lacked was me, hosting a problem-solving show called *What Would You Do?*. What most viewers did was turn off. This high-concept bit of televisual hokum involved a dilemma of some sort being posed by a member of the public, and then being given due consideration by groups of workmates. Should Mavis from Ellesmere Port leave her husband? Let's ask three good-natured lollipop ladies from Truro. Stretching the concept of 'daytime' to its very limits, it ended up being shown at 2 a.m.

Radio is where it's at. For me anyway. Here my unruly hair, imperfect teeth and raddled complexion don't matter quite so much. And my voice is fine. Not one of the greats, but fine. It's relatively inoffensive, comprehensible, not too high, not too low. My accent is what is now called accentless, which makes no sense at all. But in general, the rule is be Irish, be Scottish or be accentless.

I love radio. My love is probably dangerously close to an addiction. But I do acknowledge that the medium has developed an irritating language all of its own, and a heap of cliches to weigh it down. I know I have probably used every single cliché I'm about to mock. But I'll say one thing for me – I never hosted a regional breakfast show featuring a long-running quiz called 'What Have I Got in My Hand?'.

Let's start with time, and the sheer, unending telling of it, from us to you. Radio studios are often absurdly full of clocks. The time here, there, everywhere, ticking down and ticking away. Sometimes even local stations, getting above themselves, will have a bank of digital clocks boasting a tempting range of international times. It's 11.43 p.m. in Moscow! High time for a cuppa in Leighton Buzzard.

Speaking of Moscow, at Radio 4 we were always spun the line that Britain's nuclear submarines, out there in the murky depths, would occasionally listen to the network just to make sure that Britain was still there. So at about 2.10 p.m. on Sunday they'd hope to hear Bernard from Hayling Island putting a pertinent question to a learned panel of gardeners about soil types. Good. Fine, as you were. If instead they got someone sounding ragged and despairing and claiming to be down to their last teabag, then action was required. What sort of action is probably not for discussion here. But do sleep well.

There are many programmes in which you are guaranteed never to be more than a few seconds away from finding out what the time is. Again.

Sometimes presenters can provide a quick time-check as a neat and inoffensive way of changing the mood. Lord knows, I certainly used the trick on *Woman's Hour*, often a classic magazine-programme jumble, where they'd think nothing of following an eye-watering gynaecological discussion with seven and a half minutes precisely on 'Smokey eyeshadow – yes or no?'. Quick – just pause as though deep in thought then, in a brisk, neutral tone, tell everyone it's now 10.26 a.m., and Joanna Public surely takes a deep breath with you, uncrosses her legs, thanks her lucky stars and sticks with the programme. On we go!

The twenty-first century is awash with pomp-speak: linguistic gunge that jams up conversation and limits our understanding, while simultaneously letting too many stupid people sound like they might know what they're talking about. There is far too much of it on the radio, often allowed to go unchecked. If a fluent pomp-speaker is rightly concerned that 'stakeholders' and their 'wider client base' will require a 'suite of measures' to bring about 'real and consistent change' 'across the piece' 'going forwards', you have every right to ask why. Then you can ask what. Then you can pour yourself a stiff drink or bang your head on the desk repeatedly.

Then there are the words and phrases you never say, but often hear broadcast: spate, blaze, reveller. Now I know that sieges are no laughing matter, and you certainly need expertise to bring these tense situations to a satisfactory and peaceful conclusion. But do we need to hear about a 'trained negotiator'? Because, Lord knows, without that 'trained' we'd obviously all be imagining the implied alternative – Brenda and Brian from No. 64, the untrained but enthusiastic amateur negotiators who just fancy a crack at it with a megaphone they've picked up off eBay.

Everyone loves an animal story. The BBC local radio station I worked for had a safari park on its patch, with a media-savvy boss who could always be relied upon, especially around a bank-holiday weekend, to come up with a little something. Bernard the centipede, about to celebrate his milestone tenth birthday with a special cake; Molly the one-armed gibbon who could play 'I'm in the Mood for Dancing' on the recorder. It was harmless enough stuff – we got our 'And finally', no one was hurt, but a few more car aerials inevitably took a bit of a battering in the monkey enclosure.

Just in case there's any doubt – the best topics for a banker radio discussion include the death penalty ('I'd do the job myself,' says Reg in Tooting), cats or dogs, breast versus bottle, and the classic 'Your favourite biscuit'. If you work for commercial radio you're allowed – indeed obliged – to take a view, but pity the poor professionally even-handed BBC person who must be prepared to make a bit of a case for a Hobnob, before acknowledging that actually you can't beat a milk-chocolate digestive, and gosh, aren't gingernuts lovely when you're in the mood?

But Oh, the sheer intimacy of it all. That's what radio people tell you it has, in abundance. 'I LOVE radio – it's such an intimate medium!' Indeed. What does that mean? That you're only wearing five layers of make-up? That only eighty-nine people are listening? I don't know.

Or maybe I do. Shoving all pointless cynicism aside, there have been moments when I've felt a real connection to a contributor or a caller, or I sense that I've been part of a programme that may have made someone feel better about themselves, or perhaps less alone. And as a listener, I love to feel involved. I listen to people I like, and to people I loathe. To the irascible and the belligerent, the gentle and the companionable. I can be moved, irritated, despairing and enlightened in the space of fifteen minutes. I could give up working on radio, as long as I could keep on listening.

I also know I may be lying about this.

FI

SO. MANY. THINGS. Firstly, may I congratulate you on Garvey's Radio Personality Assessment Chart, which I confidently predict will become as legendary as the Bristol Stool Chart. And I know that is one of your secret obsessions. I think a poster of the GRPA next to every 'creativity zone' in New Broadcasting House might be the thing that keeps BBC Sounds on an even keel. Oh 'creativity zones'. Shoot me now.

Secondly, how come you got sent to see a life coach?! Isn't that the kind of thing the BBC does when no one is brave enough to take you into a room and tell you your entire team is walking out on account of your 'starry' behaviour? Or when they actually want to fire you?

I'm asking you that question in my special 'radio compassionate voice', which has a tone and timbre to it that I never use in real life, and I'm also very much enjoying asking you that question knowing that I won't actually have to listen to your answer. Because isn't it one of the fundamental attractions of being a talk show radio host? You get to ask all of the questions and decide how much of an answer you want? In fact you don't even have to listen to what the answer is at all, you can just head off into the next question, which doesn't even have to be relevant to the previous one. You can drop all the norms of conversation that you have to adhere to in the real world. And the bit that the egomaniac loves: *no one can ask any questions back*. I know! Genius! Pop that in your Control Juicer and whizz it up to ten!

Although, wouldn't it make a great programme if, just one day of the year, all the interviewees could come back at a questioner with a question of their own? Quick, write that down, it's a sure-fit hit of a show.

Thirdly (and then I'll stop with the list, mainly because I don't think there is a word 'fourthly', but I'll get a young, unfairly underpaid researcher to check that out for me during the next item and then pretend on air that I knew it all along) your assessment of the times of the day for broadcasters is very cruel and I don't want to be in the room (or do I?) when you tell Jeremy V. that his lunchtime slot makes him a 'mere companion'. One man's 'mere companion' is another man's largest news-based radio show in Europe. You really are the Mistress of Pain on the DAB dial.

The astute definitions of what those shows mean in the pecking order of the day made me think about how radio egos will fare in the world of on-demand, which our children show every sign of using more than actual radio. Not for them sitting through an edition of the *Round Britain Quiz* (after devolution a very short show) just so they can get to the more meaty PM. Do you think that the matrix will change forever and, heaven forbid, sheer numbers will prevail? Far too many shows on old-fashioned radio get counted as being listened to when in fact no one has a decent way of working out if the radio has just been left on to deter burglars (has anyone ever surveyed the burglars to find out if this works?), some-one has fallen asleep within minutes, or they've simply left the room. The advance of tech allows you to tell who started a download but found it dull and didn't finish it, who shared it because they liked it so much, who unsub-scribed because they didn't. There may be trouble ahead.

I'd also agree entirely with your sentiment about the ego that drives you towards a microphone. It is a very odd thing to want to do. Essentially it is reading out loud, but it's *go commando* reading out loud, isn't it, and there has to be a certain type of frisson about your own self-importance to believe that anyone might want to know – let alone hear – the naked workings of your inner mind. I like the notion that when the world ends all that will be left is you on top of the rubble with your loudhailer. What topics will you choose to spout forth on? Soup? Your new kitten Dora? Will you tell people more about Liverpool? I'll tell you what, if I am buried deep below it'll make it much easier just to shut my eyes and breathe out for the last time.

And yes, we broadcasters are full of oxymorons. We like the transient permanence of it all. We're not that important, but your day might well revolve around us. We want to be heard, but not every word remembered. We'll be in your kitchen for decades, but you don't actually know us. If we were in the animal kingdom, what would we be? I think maybe those monkeys with the strange bottoms? Normal from the front, disturbing from the wrong angle? I feel a phone-in coming on. I've done worse topics than that. And so have you.

Yet the minute I walked into a radio station I felt at home. Make of that what you will. And I can't be *quite* as cynical about it as you. I do think it still conveys a sincerity that no other medium manages. When it just lets people talk and tell you their stories – well it just works. It really isn't any more complicated than that. Most shows are either 'People say things' or 'People sing things'.

And we are surfing a wave right now. Audio is in the ascendant, we are in a sweet spot. Blessed by the tech that puts headphones on our ears and can deliver content to our phones, we have proved to be creative, nimble, cheap and daring and everyone wants a part of us now. I welcome this huge new audio dawn. I am enjoying riding across it on my high horse, while shouting how we were there before the sticky fingers of fame and Netflix budgets came along, and there is a craft to it you know, and you can't just pitch up from the world of TV like Patron Saint of Plunging Necklines Amanda Holden has and expect to be really good at it (although she is) and do you remember the days of magnetic tape and UHERs and . . . Oh repeat to fade . . .

Now that Harry and Meghan *and* Michelle Obama all have podcasts where they are wide-eyed with excitement at this crazy notion of being able to 'talk to people', I think we can stand back like a parent watching their child win Gold at the Olympics and feel proud of them, but also really pompously chuffed with ourselves.

So yes, we're probably a bit odd. But let's never stop, eh?

6

FORGOTTEN YOUR PASSWORD:

THE BARONESS OF DALSTON VERSUS DIGITAL NATIVES

FI

'THE FOLLOWING IS A SEVEN-MINUTE READ.'

Do you subscribe to sites and online newspapers and blogs that now tell you that? Ain't it just the strangest thing? I understand the need to have a time slot in mind if you are offering someone a Pilates class or instructing them on how to bake a cake, but how long it takes to read something? What happens if you want to break off halfway through and have a ponder? What happens if you need to move your finger under the words even more slowly while your lips catch up? What happens if you are super-speedy? And does anyone look at their watch and think: 'Actually I've only got six minutes and forty-three seconds. I won't bother.'?

It's one of many aspects of shiny, tech-driven life that send me slightly potty. So much of our new online experience is mind-expanding and glorious, but some of it is hive-inducingly grating. 'This is a seven-minute read' stirs in me a teenage spirit of rebellion that whoever wrote it can't possibly want me to have. The article-timers are probably closer to being teenagers than I am, so how very odd that it's me who feels the need to put two fingers up at them.

But if I'm past the age of teenage rebellion, why am I so full of annoyance? And what does a middle-aged rebellion even look like? You'd hope it contains something of the stuff that we have learned along the way, that it uses the powers of age and experience. If you ask me what it is that I do actually know at the age of fifty-two, the answers are quite simple:

- Don't ever buy a polyester jumper, no matter how good it looks in the shop – one wash and it's gone.
- Nearly every childhood drama can be solved by a tickle under the armpits followed by a really strong hug.
- And although we are attracted to people for their strengths, it is their weaknesses that ultimately make us love them.

Apart from the polyester warning, it boils down to two things, doesn't it: the Power of Love and the Power of Silly.

How might we fare if we tried to use these powers as weapons in the constant, slappy little fifty-something fist fight I appear to be having with a modern world that has crept up on me?

I'd like to start by gifting to you my all-time favourite small rebellious act, which you can undertake without leaving your house, manning a picket-line brazier or even signing a petition. It lies in the drop-down menu of titles you get every time you make a purchase online or register for some service you may or may not need. I used to just obey orders and was always just Miss F, Glover, but then I realised you can choose to be whoever you like. Some only offer you the choice of Mr, Mrs, Ms and Miss, but some are luxurious, ranging from Duke and Duchess all the way through to Monsignor via a couple of Captains. I've even seen a Cardinal up there. Don't go worrying that there's some kind of code of naming and shaming that will immediately render your custom void. No one gives a monkeys what you say until you get to the payment page, and so over the last few years I've used and abused the options available and then taken small satisfaction in receiving parcels from bewildered delivery drivers addressed to Brigadier Sir Field Marshall Glover, Baroness Fiona of Dalston and John Lewis only knows me as Miss FedUp O'Forms.

There's also a train I take to see my mum in Swindon on which the operator's page comes up as soon as I log on. It addresses me by the name I once put in. It should say Welcome Fi. But whenever I sit down in a cramped, backward-facing seat for the heady fifty-three minutes of fun-time travel through suburbia it says Welcome Sucker. It makes me happy every time.

I should warn you that this does all become a tad problematic when you try to physically mix the old world with the new. I got caught out when I tried to pick up a case of wine from Majestic and they wouldn't release it because I had no form of physical ID in the name of Dr No Bollocks. The expression on the young man's face was priceless and suggested that just for a nanosecond – no more and no less than that – I'd broken through the trope of the middle-aged woman.

Please, please can we talk about this out-of-date trope? You can probably picture the middle-aged woman of popular imagination immediately. Slightly crumpled, strangely depleted, a bit confused and definitely a bit fed up. In an identity line-up – where the crime is simply Getting Through Life – she'd be in a mid-calf-length skirt, her hair would need some attention, she'd probably be clutching a capacious handbag and a virtue-signalling tote bag and, as a fresh addition for this century, she'd be peering at a piece of technology, stabbing at a phone or tutting at a laptop.

It's way beyond its sell-by date. Our calf-length skirts are more likely to be ankle-skimming skinny jeans. Our hair can be a more vibrant chemical version of what our younger follicles managed to produce naturally. Handbag, you say? I've got one of those slung-across-the-shoulder packs because I travel so lightly through life, darlings. But yes – that phone, Oh that bloody phone, the cause of so much rage and confusion. That is the only part of the trope that, I'll admit, rings true.

Don't dismiss this as a Luddite rant, because I love what technology has brought us. I enjoy working with it on a daily basis in my job, and on the home front it has totally saved my bacon. Just this morning I've sorted school-dinner payments online, filled up the fridge, joined in a really funny chat with other mums whom – now the kids are at secondary school – I simply wouldn't ever have got to meet in person. Later today, a kind friend has promised to send me a bouncy new playlist on Spotify that I would never have been able to access before. But for all my adult life I have felt that, when it comes to technology, I am running to stay just slightly ahead of the storm. And it's exhausting.

Ours is the generation which has given birth to the digital natives. We ourselves were born as analogue creatures. We are the last generation not to have experienced a childhood full of social-media feeds and apps, of 'drops' and the opportunity to look at whatever we want, when we want and discard it when we don't. But we are also the generation that can't expect to be forgiven for not understanding it. It can almost feel as if the tech moan is as old as the hills – or as old as Windows 95, as the kidz would say. It's not if you look at the long passage of time, but it does render the childhood experience of a fifty-something to a disproportionately faraway bin of history. That can sometimes feel a little cruel. Just look at the things that have happened in our adult lives:

The internet itself arrived in 1991. I was twenty-two.

I attempted to book my first holiday on lastminute. com in 1998. I was twenty-nine. I was thirty by the time most of the pages had loaded.

Facebook, or TheFacebook as it was originally called, only came into existence in 2004. I was thirty-five.

I have jars of chutney in my fridge that are older than Tinder, and some smoked mackerel pâté that's got a good few years on TikTok.

But now, 95 per cent of Europe is online, as is 60 per cent of the global population. Four billion people every day have to face the fact that they've probably forgotten their password. A third of those online are aged eighteen to thirty-five, but a quarter are forty-five to sixty-five and that makes me want to congratulate fifty-somethings around the world.

We've done well, because in our lifetime we have had to navigate our way through a massive revolution of thought and process, using only our thumbs and a universal charger. If you have never known any other way of living, then of course it must be easier to exist in this highly advanced world, but we have had to make massive changes. On a wet Saturday afternoon our young ones have YouTube, Snapchat, WhatsApp, GarageBand, PS4 and the rest. We had Dickie Davies's *World of Sport*. There can be no more profound comparison and I'm surprised it's not mentioned more.

We've long acknowledged that we are the sandwich generation. Having kids later in life, and having parents who live so much longer, places many of us in that position of enduring/enjoying two decades of double caring responsibilities. And now we also exist as tech sandwiches, too. We've lived our lives with one foot on the dock of the bay and one foot on the boat trying to leave. Precarious, isn't it?

That duality seeps into your psyche. I don't think I'll be alone in feeling that although I present to the outside world the image of someone who is thriving in the digital world, I'm actually living my life in an almost perpetual state of flux.

In my household, my relative technological ineptitude has created a strange balance of power. Far too frequently I have had to ask my kids (who are now teenagers) to help me out with all elements of connectivity. It's a decisive change from my own parental relationships. The phrase 'Can you help me with this' was literally never uttered to me by either of my parents. There was nothing in their world that they needed my help with. At the age of eleven I was unlikely to be of any use fixing the exhaust on the car, banging in some shelving at the weekend, or wiring up a speaker for a turntable. But now . . . good God, there is so much I simply am not able to do without the help of a child.

The worst offender has to be that thing on the TV where you have to plod across an alphabet with your remote control in order to tap in your LoWer Case! password, the one you thought back in 2017 you'd never forget. Yup. Guess what? You did. Nothing – not even sudden childbirth without pain relief – makes me more angry. Then there's the bit where they send a code to a totally different device so you can get back into the device that you are on? I am often on that second device because I can't find the first. Round and round and round we go in a never-ending loop of three-word questions that are always displayed as statements – and, yes, that drives me up the wall, too. Surely they are questions? Forgotten Your Password. Remind me Tomorrow. Launch Without Updating. Don't they need a question mark after them?

On far too many occasions my kids have had to gently take the remote away from their seething mother in a table-turning moment of family responsibility. Although I am enormously grateful to them, it gives them a sense of power and knowledge that is then quite hard to remove from other areas of life. When I tell them actual facts about how drinking half a bottle of vodka just will knock out a lot of brain cells forever, or why posting THAT on Tik Tok might come back to haunt them – well they just feel they have a superior sense of the world because yesterday Mum couldn't connect Spotify to the kitchen speaker, so what would she know about delayed gratification, privacy, stamina and resilience?

While I may feel powerless in the face of domestic technology and teen competence, this ambient power of youth is never more apparent than at work.

There used to be a time when a new person would join the team of a BBC programme and be introduced as 'This is Gareth, he's just come back from ten years as Beirut correspondent, he's done some cracking stuff about the break-up of the Balkans too, he speaks Spanish and started out as an adviser to Shirley Williams.'

Now it's just 'Welcome Luke. He's twenty-eight.'

There is nothing I can do about so much of this because, rightly, Luke, at twenty-eight, is here to stay. His synapses are wired for the modern world, he feels comfortable in it. The difference between me and him is profound because he has always experienced tech first and the physical second. He has the confidence I don't.

Or didn't.

On finding myself single at the age of fifty, I spent a couple of years sinking into my sofa of an evening like one of those flat, flabby fishes on the seabed. I sought refuge and safety in staying very still, camouflaged against the cushions thinking, 'If I just don't move, no one will threaten my existence,' and that worked fine for a while. Once I could finally operate the remote control, I did what most couples my age are probably doing on a Saturday night anyway – I watched endless box sets, while pouring wine. I did myself proud. I excelled at it. I watched French box sets, Italian ones, one from Belgium, and the obvious Scandinavian ones. I was like my own Saturday night TV Schengen agreement. I got lost in the clichés – the French ones always have to have young guys zooming round on mopeds selling drugs. The Italian ones always have a sensationally beautiful sex worker living in a tower block who gets brutally murdered in the first ten minutes. She has the kind of beauty that would have opened doors to employment in all manner of areas – banking, finance, publishing – but hey, let's stick with another tired old trope, shall we?

But after a while that got boring, and as my wonderful theatre friend Debs says, 'The only way to the bar is through the show.' The only modern way out of Saturday night solo TV-surfing back into the real world of people and potential partnerships seemed to lie in mastering the ability to use a dating app. I needed to join Luke's world, where you put the tech first and the physical second. Would you like to shimmy up to a fact and ask it to dance? By 2037, more than half of all babies born in the UK will be to couples who met online. Boom. Online matchmaking is just the accepted way now to light that touchpaper in the hope of affinity leading to attraction, leading to someone who has a BTEC in commitment, leading to 'forever'. In fact, all of that is just an algorithm by another name, isn't it?

Obviously, I was not going to ask my kids to help me with posting a profile, getting my settings right, learning how to hide my page so I could flick through blokes who can't flick through me (ladies, you can ALWAYS find a way to do this). By jiminy, it turned out that I could actually do it. I could flip my brain to work the way the digital native's does when there was a real imperative to do it.

And so we get a big tick on the implementation of The Power of Love, but back to The Power of Silly for a moment because we're not done with that yet. Why not also have some moments of fun messing with your search algorithm? Why fence yourself into a concentric circle of being sold more of the same all the time? Isn't it daft that the more we shop and the more we search, the tighter the concentric circles get, as every company learns more about our choices and simply sends more of the same our way. Why not flex your last old-fashioned bicep of choice and pop some left-field propositions into your search engine? I like to think this leaves some friend of Luke's scratching his hipster beard while sitting at his bright white desk outside Mountain View thinking, 'But we have her down as organic vegetable boxes and smoke-less fuel for the wood-burner, why is she looking at foie gras and penthouses in Dubai?'

And get your kicks where you can. Press the Launch Without Updating option whenever possible. It's the thing that comes up all the time on our TV, or on an app for food delivery or paying for those school dinners. It just means some coder somewhere wants you to justify his (and, trust me, it is usually a his) faster and shinier version of the thing you'd only just got used to using. But I don't want to be updated all the time. I don't always need to go faster and be shinier and have more connectivity; sometimes it's OK to just want to pause. By the time you are fifty, 'pausing' is also on the list of hobbies and interests. It might even be my favourite pastime. Just for a moment, take the chance to stay still in a world you might never have wished to be as fast as it always will be now.

And in case you are left wondering, I have done a lot of swiping away. Any man pictured at the top of a mountain or boasting about how they come first all the time. Anyone taking themselves too seriously. Anyone who 'likes a long walk and a Sunday pub lunch', because that's just a cliché too far.

And anyone in a polyester jumper, obvs, because it shows that you really haven't done much of your own washing, otherwise you too would know how foolhardy that purchase has been.

By the way, this took about seventeen hours to write. Read it at whatever speed you like.

JANE

WHAT THE GOOD BARONESS OF DALSTON needs to understand is how much harder all this is for me. She is merely unsure of her place in the digital world, but I know I simply don't belong here. I am five important years her senior, and they really count. I still jab at a keyboard; I'm tentative, even fearful – I'll never sail across the keys, trusting in it all, totally at ease.

I endured Computer Studies – forty minutes a week – in my last year at school, in 1981. The lessons consisted almost entirely of some confusing blether about binary numbers, delivered, droningly, by somebody who didn't have much faith in what they were saying. It was all entirely theoretical. The school didn't have any computers. The closest I had to a handheld device was my invaluable calculator. I remember showing it to my grandmother, then in her late seventies, who was nonplussed by it: 'You're allowed to take this into the examination?!'

Like Fi, I have had to turn to my own digital natives to assist in the home. I'm not saying they were solely responsible for setting up the parental controls, but they played a part, certainly. I too have had my moments of gentle subversion: I was briefly the Very Reverend Jane Garvey with British Telecom. I must say, it did feel pretty good. Take that, telecoms giant with annual profits of £22,905m!

Like almost every member of my just-about-Boomer generation, I rail against change and talk wistfully of the high street while ordering doormats and catnip toys on Amazon. I Accept All Cookies at least eight or nine times a day, without ever really knowing what that means. Although the language strikes me as moronic – 'cookie', for heaven's sake – why is this stuff both so infantile and so toxic?

Of course, the modern isn't new. Somebody, somewhere, must have been the first person to be really good on the lute, for example. I say 'person', but I think we all know it will have been a man, with time on his hands. And I dare say his family and friends will have missed the relative peace before he got twanging. If I live long enough, I may witness my grandchildren casually 3D-printing a submarine with a squadron of avatars while their parents reminisce about Nintendo DS. Will I ever see moving pavements? No – not at this rate. They're the elusive unicorns of the future, promised for as long as anyone can remember, but still stubbornly confined to international airports.

What I do have, in my connected world, is that omnipresent fuzz of tension. I cannot escape it. My phone knows where I am, and yet I panic beyond all measure if I don't know where *it* is. In the 1970s – and Fi's right, it may as well be a thousand years ago – the phone was in the bloody hall, for God's sake!

Algorithms have me sewn up – they know I like elasticated-waist trousers that look as though they're not. They know I'm single, and I hear regularly about Great Funeral Plans in my area. In all honesty, our generation's getting off lightly here. Thirty-year-old women are blitzed by advertising by the egg-freezing industry. I've just got my own mortality to contemplate, but they're under pressure to produce even more eager consumers.

So I'm trapped. I'm someone who'd be perfectly content reading by candlelight – as long as there was universal suffrage and I had a decent pair of varifocals. But tech has me in its grasp. It confounds and cushions me, somehow making me anxious, dull-witted and over-informed, all at once. What it hasn't gifted me yet is someone in ill-fitting outdoor gear who likes long walks and a pub lunch.

7

CONGRATULATIONS ON YOUR DIVORCE!:

SOLO PARENTING AND SEPARATION STATIONERY

JANE

AN ELDERLY COUPLE AND I sit in a stuffy sitting room, all doilies and ornamental windmills. I'm in a hurry and I'm hungry. There may be a link. I'm also here under false pretences. It's becoming clear to me that this cranky, thin-lipped pair are not happily married at all, and yet here I am, trying to make a cockle-warming radio feature to mark the occasion of their diamond wedding anniversary. (Yes, it was a quiet week – what of it?)

If in doubt as an interviewer, never try anything original. I suppose I could modify the old classic 'What's the secret to a long and happy marriage?' and just ask 'What's the secret to a long marriage?'.

But that seems a bit cowardly. And besides, there's an easy answer to that one – a sure-fire way to ensure a long marriage is simply to stay married. Some of you have managed exactly that.

Now press on, intrepid young reporter. You're not Kate Adie yet, but we all have to start somewhere.

'What's the secret to a long and happy marriage?'

Him: 'Eh?'

Her: 'What she say?'

Me, booming: 'WHAT'S THE SECRET TO A LONG AND HAPPY MARRIAGE?'

Silence. I may remind you that in these circumstances it is customary for someone to oblige the inquisitor by dutifully serving up, 'Never go to bed on a row,' then you might hope for a reference to compromise – 'I just do what I'm told!' says the twinkly old gent, and moves on to a jokey aside about letting her have the last word. That's how it's done. Then the reporter's secured her golden nuggets of wisdom; she can breathe a sigh of relief and, after some routine niceties ('Look at these lovely flowers!!'), bolts for the exit, mind on a roast-pork bap. With stuffing, no apple sauce.

But not on this occasion. The stale whiff of acrimony hung in the air. Compromise clearly had no place here; there had been many a night of seething after a ritual ding-dong; the last word had yet to be uttered. Sixty years of this. I drove away disheartened, after finally securing a few minutes' of just-about-broadcastable rumination. I saw them again the next week on page nine of the local newspaper, side by side in their identical armchairs, almost smiling, and happy enough. Happy . . . enough. Strange phrase that one. Quite weighty. Still together, still married.

And that's not easy to do. Many of us don't even get close to it. These days it's not the calamity it used to be – you're not a social pariah, exactly. Though, as many a divorced woman can testify, you're not as socially sought after as the 'spare man'. He's really handy. You're sometimes entertaining, in a world-weary sort of way, but logistically you're a wee bit of an inconvenience at the dinner table. There can sometimes be quite a flap about where to seat you, as though you might start weeping, or launch yourself at any hapless male over the smoked-salmon starter unless you're tethered down to your chair with a heavy rope.

No, no, officially, divorce isn't an issue any more. There's even a rather half-hearted attempt to make the whole business something you might want to celebrate. You can buy a cheeky card to send a chum: 'Happy Divorce Day, he was an arse' says one, showing a woman in her bridal finery, a supportive friend on each side, and the figure of a man in a tuxedo lying on the floor. Is he dead? Whodunnit? On another – 'Congratulations on your divorce!' – a woman drives off into the sunset at the wheel of a convertible, accompanied by a sizeable dog. What's the betting Gloria Gaynor's belting out her signature anthem? You go, girl!

Yes, I'm afraid there are more tasteless options, too; rib-ticklers like 'Your vagina deserves better' and its even more juvenile-sounding chum, 'Your willy deserves better anyway.' Good grief, chaps. You're a grown-up, you've got a significant and painful relationship break-up behind you, say penis!!! Although, honestly, can you think of any straight man you know popping into a card shop to mark the occasion of his mate's divorce? Oh, poor Clive! He must be going through all sorts of hell. I'll just see if Paperchase has got anything to ease his pain, Oooh yes, that's just the thing!

No. That doesn't happen. So, on the whole, these cards are, like almost all cards, for women to send to other women. And therefore the men on these cards are always the arses, and the women are liberated and apparently blameless, free to roam the world with large dogs.

I'm sorry to say it's not quite that simple, and – incredibly – women can be monumental arses, too. Of course, not quite as often, she adds hastily. I don't want to lose the sisterhood here.

A good, meaty divorce is a hugely underrated spectator sport. OK, there's no catering and people tend not to dress up, but it goes on much, much longer than any major fixture and, as long as you're not an active participant, it won't cost you a penny. Really very good value all round.

The important thing as a spectator is to be close enough to get the all the intel, without actually having a responsibility to any of the individuals directly involved. A good friend of a good friend of someone having an absolutely terrible time is about the right sort of distance. That way, you might hear some of the messy detail, but have no obligation to enter the emotional fray yourself, armed with Kleenex and a bottle of that not-inexpensive extra-dry Prosecco, or spend hours sitting at the other end of a crumb-strewn sofa (where did she get those cushions?) while a red-eyed woman tells you exactly the same anecdotes she told you last week. Only in this week's version of events his behaviour is considerably worse, and she emerges, miraculously, with more credit than ever.

But let's say you are that red-eyed woman. You haven't slept for a month and you're living on small sponge puddings and ready-made custard. Lank hair, complexion at maximum blotch, that awful T-shirt again. But you haven't cracked yet, and you won't, as it turns out. You're getting up, you're getting on, but this, truly, is as hard as it's ever been.

It can be horribly addictive, though. Being the star of your own six-part drama. On you roll, thinking and rethinking, half-remembering and reinventing. You're almost certain to find a receptive audience; in fact, in some ways you've never been more popular. Not that this stuff is uncomplicated – you desperately need support, but sometimes your friends' willingness to wholeheartedly agree with every word you say can take your breath away. What – he really was that bad? And you always thought so? Hang on a moment . . . I thought . . .

And in the middle of another night, the realisation that those people who never cared much for you – well, they're now quite free to say so, too. Ouch. Don't overthink this, said the woman who overthought this. It is a psychological cul-de-sac, and you deserve to reclaim your rightful place on the freeway. (By which I mean an unexpectedly clear run down the M40 on a beautiful morning in May.)

The ripple effect is real – people are forced not just to take sides but to take stock, to analyse their own relationships, and be truly glad or start panicking. What – YOU two split up? You've well and truly let the side down. As someone said to me: 'I can't believe it. You're nowhere near as unhappy as us.'

But maybe that wasn't true. It takes time to acknowledge that something isn't working. Time, and courage. Sometimes, other people who care about you try to suggest there might be an issue, and you hate the fact that they're right, so make a determined if ultimately forlorn attempt to forget what they said. And a more successful attempt to be absolutely livid with them for their barefaced cheek. And when, exactly, did they become so perceptive?

Days, weeks and months are easy enough to fill in a marriage. Intimacy and indifference shouldn't really go so well together, but they often do. What did people with nothing left to say to each other do before the box set?

Meanwhile, you've got your resentment to keep you warm at night. Not an attractive emotion, that one. None of the kudos of jealousy or passion; there's no drama, no real energy. It has a bitter quality, an aftertaste, it takes you nowhere but propels you along at the same time.

No, *I'm* more tired than *you*. That game's a battle to the death, and most of us have played it. In its simplest form: I've been out at work all day, I'm knackered. I've been at home all day, I'm exhausted. And the winner is . . .?

I think you can make the case that parenting alone is easier. Maybe it was easier for me. I know I may well have been too territorial, too eager to claim the cloak of maternal martyrdom for myself. But when the buck stops, and stops with you, it's amazing how much less stressful life becomes. All the carping has gone, along with a lot of other stuff – not all of it bad. If you happened to have been married to someone who made a great cup of tea, say so. We should be allowed to own the happy memories, too.

The post-split reckoning means you lose friends, you gain friends and sometimes you regain friends, too. You can now stop pretending things are fine – and you start to notice when other people are trying to pull off your old tricks; nothing to see here, thanks. Everything's just great! Rictus grins all round. Maybe I should say something . . .? But best not. I don't want to spare them decades of married bliss.

I'm no poster girl for divorce. It's not all fun. You think about the past a lot, but you also mourn the future you won't share. You have to face the fact that the comfort blanket of the steady family life you had as a child will not be something your own children experience. You have, frankly, failed.

Perhaps it *should* feel like failure. Perhaps other people did better, or tried harder, for longer. You have nothing to boast about here. Even if there are no children, I doubt many people take it lightly. It's tough. Nor is single parenthood, even with all the material advantages

I had, something I could heartily recommend. When the children were young there were plenty of long, solitary evenings after they'd gone to bed, and occasional ragged nights of clammy childhood viruses, spilling the last dose of sticky pink Calpol all over the duvet cover at 3.17 a.m. and wanting to cry. It simply must be easier if there are two of you.

And I had it ridiculously easy. We don't hear enough from single parents caring for children with special needs – but when we do, their testimony is so powerful and should make all of us sit up, pay attention and give thanks. I heard a woman who'd called a radio station on a Saturday morning in the first lockdown spring as I was trudging round the park. She hadn't seen or spoken to anyone apart from her child for weeks; he was on the autistic spectrum and she had absolutely no way of explaining the new restrictions to him. They might go for a drive. It might calm him down; it might not. He didn't sleep much. Tomorrow would be the same, and so would the day after that.

There are nearly 2 million single parents in the UK, and we don't get the credit we deserve. I know it's hard to define a 'single parent' in the first place. Many would say, perhaps justifiably, that I had no claim to the title at all. Strictly speaking, it is 'a person bringing up a child or children without a partner'. Sounds simple enough, but circumstances vary enormously. Though most of us didn't start off this way, or ever really imagine we'd end up here. The insulting old trope of a single mother as mini-skirted minx on the make, a chain-smoking drain on the state, zoning in on that 'free council flat' is palpable nonsense. And plenty of men are single parents, too – some, like lots of women, for a good part of every week. There are widows and widowers. People who have chosen to be single parents. Some have practical and financial help from partners past and present. Others rely on their own parents. Some are completely alone. We are all getting on with it. We're not saints. If not the norm – yet – we are very normal. Our children are charming, belligerent, adorable and a pain in the backside, much like anyone else's.

And please let's not pretend that every child growing up in the much-fetishised nuclear family is guaranteed a perfect start, either. Father may smoke a pipe and look the part, but for all we know he's more interested in his fossil collection than the family. Mother may make the most wonderful sponge cakes, but be having it away with the churchwarden. Some couples may well make up a fantastic parenting unit; others consist of two self-obsessed idiots, neither of whom you'd choose to care for a child, a cheese plant, or the Year 4 gerbil over the Easter holidays.

Still worse, perhaps, to be the child trapped with a warring couple who won't, or can't, split up – it's not the cheapest option, after all. I can see why you'd have a go at staying together 'for the sake of the children', but I imagine that's not ideal if they're aware that's exactly what you're doing. And I don't know how you keep it from them.

If you're going to split up, you do have options. You can be bitter and angry for weeks, months, or the rest of your life if you like. Trust me, no one will stop you. But your children only have one childhood and, as you know, this is it. You can make it as uncertain and difficult as you like, or swallow your pride occasionally and make it bearable, even good. It's grandmothers and egg-sucking, obviously, this stuff, and I reserve the right not always to follow my own rules.

I only know enough about marriage to know I know very little. Living with another person's demands, obsessions or idiosyncrasies for decade after decade is something I don't think I could ever have done, if I'm really honest. I'm not sure I'd expect anyone to put up with mine, either. Maybe that old couple were perfectly content in their mutual antipathy. Perhaps the first forty-five years had been brilliant, and the last fifteen had been a bit of a struggle. Still – what an incredible achievement. Look, they could have been making mad, passionate love fifteen minutes before I arrived, or three minutes after I left, for all I know. More than happy enough.

FI

I WONDER WHAT HAPPENS to marriage and its hitch-hiking friend divorce – 'Got room for me in the back?' – in a future when already 42 per cent of marriages in the UK end with legal separation. The average length of the marriage that precedes that divorce is only twelve years. It doesn't look good for matrimony.

If you were looking to buy a golf club or a gym and you saw that nearly half the membership asked to leave after just over a decade, I wonder if you'd think it was a viable business proposition? I think you'd decide to take a look at alpaca-farming instead or you'd calmly read the balance sheet, accept what might happen, and adjust your expectations accordingly. The unique nature of marriage, though – being the public statement of a very private thing – means we enter into it with very little sense of what might happen based on 'other people', because at the time it feels as if it's just for us. But the killer fact is that if you invite people to the wedding, they feel entitled to come to the divorce, too.

Given the high statistics for divorce, I'm surprised there aren't *more* merchandising opportunities, Jane. Where are the key fobs and the T-shirts and the bumper stickers and the themed mini-breaks? That speaks to the 'shame' that I think we are *meant* to feel if divorce enters our lives. Of course it is sad. I'm not denying that. Heaven knows, I have spent too many years of my own life reduced to 'Human Only Just Functioning – Level 1' by it. It is the end of something that started out with so much joyful promise. But the prurient nature of some people's attitude to divorce is rather mean and strange and perhaps needs to shove itself up its proverbial aisle and reflect the reality a bit more, doesn't it? Because there simply is a lot of divorce about. I remember hearing a journalist trying to dig around in an interview with Björn from Abba about his split with Agnetha – the implication being that their lives must be shattered ruins of what they could have been – to which he just shrugged and said, 'No, not really – it's Sweden.'

I was left thinking that this might be some kind of a coded answer to all difficult questions in the world, but in fact it is true that in societies where divorce rates have been high for some time, divorce is simply not viewed in the same way any more. Norway and Sweden both adopted the no-fault divorce decades ago, and after the Second World War embraced more permissive attitudes to marriage and relationships full stop. Most Western countries now have similar divorce rates to these Nordic giants but still lag behind in actual attitudes to splitting up.

There is more to it, obviously. In Northern Europe there tends to be a greater sense of the state being behind the individual – higher taxes providing better social services – which has meant a move away from total reliance on family life as the ultimate support network. And the whole Nordic region can boast power surges in terms of gender equality. The autonomy that comes with giving women a life outside the home – and the way that reshapes the family – definitely has its part to play in how marriage is seen. And now, if anyone would like me to stop sounding like an 11 a.m. radio documentary on the history of the affidavit, just shout loudly from the back.

Oh, OK.

So why don't we just accept that divorce is with us as a part of life for many, many people – myself included – so it might be time to leave behind this notion that it is a source of gossipy intrigue, a cacophony of failings, something that jolts everyone's sense of love and togetherness – maybe we just say, 'Are you OK?', actually listen to the answer and move on. Digging around in someone else's pain so you can feel better about your own fate ain't no way to do business, although unfortunately it is exactly a way to do newspaper business, as every tabloid knows. You are the tabloids if you buy the tabloids, so we all have a part to play in that.

But all logic goes out of the window when it comes to protecting the kids. It's amazing how the same people who like to chat and scurry and gossip and tut about your separation are the same people whose first question is 'How are the kids?', as if you hadn't thought of it every single waking second of every single day. And quite a few of the nights, too. It's almost as if they would *like* to hear that collateral damage has been done. But in my experience, which includes being the child of a divorce or two, it is not a given that parents who separate automatically take their kids' hopes and dreams away with them. If what kids see is you hanging on in there because it pleases other people, or starving yourself of oxygen up on High Moral Ground Hill, or if you are taking emotional or even physical pain from someone, or inflicting it on them – or you hope that one day Jane

Garvey will turn up with her trusty mic and confer on you the accolade of a whole slot on Radio Wyvern's *Late Teatime News Show* – well . . . er . . . maybe that's not the stuff of a terrific childhood. If we are able to, don't we try and make sure our kids don't stay at the scene of an accident any longer than they have to?

It is not for us to tell our kids how happy or unhappy their childhood has been. It is for them to tell us. And I am sure they will. A frequent refrain in my house already (along with 'Really? Hot sauce with that, too?') is that the kids will no doubt make a better job of all aspects of their lives, and I am genuinely looking forward to watching them do so. I think it probably is the kindest thing you can do as a parent, to let your kids overtake you. But perhaps that is me trying to assuage my guilt over never being able to invite them to the diamond wedding anniversary.

Later in life they may well head over to Oslo or Stockholm, where I'll be living my best life with my sizeable dogs (yes I did spot that phrase, you unkind sister), to have the 'It's not working' chat, because it is true that children of divorce are more likely to get divorced themselves. If they come to me when they are adults saying that their marriage was no longer a source of happiness, I wouldn't immediately send them to a lawyer, but I also wouldn't tell them to stay in it. Would you? But I don't think we condemn them to that fate simply by being divorced ourselves. Plenty of friends who came from what seemed to be stable homes have struggled with marriage, too. If all you have seen of a long-term relationship is the ease with which your parents have sailed through it, then maybe it is hard to know how to deal with the stormy bits yourself. I believe, to use an analogy from another sport I don't actually partake in, that the best sailors are the ones who have seen rough seas.

I hear you on the Calpol conundrum. Parenting alone is easier in daylight hours. It's often just easier with an audience. Younger friends now do clever things to get through the nights and the isolation – I know of one who is in a WhatsApp group called the 3 a.m. Club. When they're up on a night feed they see if anyone else is around. How comforting is that? And if part of the reason for Norway's high divorce rate is simply that other support networks have helped to take away the need to rely solely on one person for your backup, it will be very interesting to see where our new interlaced-through-tech life takes parenting.

I can't help feeling that we are about to enter a rollercoaster of change on the long-term relationship front. Individualism is the modern way – which is probably fine until you have kids, and then I would imagine it is rubbish. Parenting is no place for thought processes that simply begin and end with you. And a relationship into which you bring small, dependent and time-consuming creatures definitely needs malleability – on all sides.

In case you need some more statistics – guess what, I have some. The weak bits of marriage are between one and two years (oops – we've got on the wrong train, let's get off at the first station) and eleven and twelve years (oops – we've arrived at the destination. It's not as advertised.). I don't get a prize for this – but I have done both of these things. To some people this will define my life. I would like that not to be the case. Not least because I don't really want to be a woman whose reputation exists through how it worked out, or not, with a man. And also let's be honest here Jane, we are fortunate if we are emotionally and financially able to stand on our own two feet. Many people aren't so lucky. But like you, I can do the long night of the self-aware/destructive soul. There is a dangerously fine line between those two things, and although it is definitely liberating to realise your failures, I'd be a muppet if I didn't admit that I am also envious of those in safe and loving relationships where they are simply never going to have to do that. Where failure simply lies rather comfortably in the for poorer/in sickness/worse side of the marital bed.

Having given it not inconsiderable thought, it seems to me that there isn't a secret to a long and happy marriage – all the clichés of not going to bed on a row, or he always does the bins, I do the gardening or whatever – that's not it. That's *someone's* marriage somewhere, but it probably wasn't yours and it definitely wasn't mine. You can't have a marriage *like* anybody else's.

So I'm not even going to refer your case to The Court of Emotional Justice. I put it to you that you didn't stay married – but that is no crime. And you don't have to stay divorced. It is a legal process, not a definition of the rest of your life.

Don't beat yourself up. The example you set your kids is awesome. A woman who really went for it at something she was – and still is – good at. Someone with decent friends. A sense of humour. Solvent. Funny. Capable with a chickpea. Sometimes very odd. Certainly indomitable.

Good enough? Yes, you absolutely are.

8

SLIPPING INTO MIDDLE AGE:

KNITWEAR, BATHMATS AND HAS ANYONE SEEN MY OLD AGE?

FI

I DON'T KNOW IF I want to get old. Not just older, but really old. I know I should want to. I do know what the alternative is. And I know it offends people when I say that I don't, because if you have lost someone too soon it seems careless and unempathetic for anyone to wish themselves away. But I'm not doing that – I am simply admitting that, in my mind's eye, my own old age doesn't feature as it seems to for other people. I'm sorry if that is an uncomfortable thing to say. I'm interested as to why, just as I'd be interested in anything where the consensus of opinion the world over seems to be that this is a thing I shouldn't be thinking. The good innings, the ripe old age, the celebratory telegram – this is the right direction of travel. Whenever I have dared to utter a sense of my own quite short longevity, people have tried to argue me out of it. Unsuccessfully, mind you, because it is still stubbornly there. My inability to grasp a sense of my own geriatric phase might have quite a lot to do with the vision of it around me; it's very different

133

to how other phases of life beckoned me on when I was much younger.

For instance, middle age, which presented itself rather well from the vantage point of youth, promising a life that would just be more comfortable, balanced. It was a place where you could hear the wind rustling through the trees. And where you might actually consider 'just going out for a walk' so that you could hear that.

I was looking forward to it.

By its very definition, the concept of middle age ran along different lines to youth or old age – the two book-ends of life it finds itself in between. In my mind it had its own style and rules and logic and pace. At the week-end, middle-aged people said things like 'I must go and fill the car up.' This was a trip in itself – not something that you did in desperation when the needle was right on zero. Middle-aged people never went to the garage just to buy a packet of Marlboro Lights and a can of Diet Coke (never the tempting Yorkie bar, though, because we all knew that was just for truckers).

A middle-aged person might 'pop into town on Saturday to get a shoe mended' and call that a trip, too. This was remarkable on both fronts – that you could get a shoe mended, and that you'd think that was what a Saturday was for.

Middle-aged people looked different. They had clothes, not outfits, hair, not hairstyles, and they had lives with routines in them. You didn't see them staggering around after midnight, vomiting on insecurity and Jägerbombs and suffering from DontNeedACoat-itis – the unique young person's illness, yet to be cured by simply wearing a jumper.

Ageing was the inevitable way out of the mad, in-secure planet of youth, when it mattered more than life itself what Debbie thought of your puffball skirt/ choice of boyfriend/summer-holiday hair. Middle age was also attractive because it always seemed a very long way off.

There was plenty of time to be something else before you came to rest in its welcoming embrace. According to TV and magazines – my only real sources of news about the outside world – you had about twenty years to decide your fate, choose your job or profession, find a place to live. You'd absolutely know who you were by then, and also what you liked to do. You could stand in front of that newsagent's rack of life and instantly reach for *Power Tool Monthly* if DIY had taken your fancy – or *Simply Crochet* if that had hooked you in. You could make weak jokes like that and someone might actually laugh. You'd not be in a quandary thinking *could* I like techno? If I just took up rock-climbing, my life *would* have more meaning. Shit, maybe I *should* go and live in Shropshire.

Catalogues that flopped through the letterbox sug-gested a laughter-filled middle-aged life, one in which the problem of being cold had been solved with a lot of woollens. Even in summer these catalogues kept coming with their jumpers, wraps and tank tops, pages and pages of the things. Jumpers were clearly huge enablers, because once armed with them you could take cruises where you might bump into lots of other happy midlifers who were also wrapped up warm, too. You could afford to take cruises because underneath your jumpers you were wearing nothing but a final-salary pension scheme. This raunchy little image can no longer be mentioned to a contemporary fifty-something because it is so far beyond our wildest financial dreams.

These smiling people were always part of a couple – even though statistically that is unlikely (see previous chapter). And these couples would always have a drink in their hands, although their faces would show none of the signs of daily alcohol abuse.

Oldish people on TV were especially appealing. TV was considered terribly wrong for kids in our household and the limits on watching it were severe, which of course just meant that whatever I *did* watch was branded into my very heart. If you are only allowed one lollipop you are going to savour every moment of it.

And so *The Gentle Touch*, *Juliet Bravo*, *Dallas* and *Dynasty* took on a significance way beyond what even the most devoted of scriptwriters can have imagined. They offered very different views of what forty-something people did with their time, but each had their own place of merit. I was particularly fond of the positively mundane plot lines of *Juliet Bravo*. Dodgy roofers on the prowl but about to, literally, slip up? Man collecting for 'charity' seem vaguely familiar, and not in a good way?

Inspector Jean Darblay fought low-level crime in very sensible shoes and always won despite the male prejudice she constantly suffered, which was served up somewhere between humour and pathos with no hope of change. How prescient.

As for *Dallas* and *Dynasty* – if I close my eyes and try to recall any plot I simply can't, but what I do see are endless parties where skinny, slightly vulnerable women are being played off against each other. They're wearing full make-up even at breakfast. There are men marching around a lot being loud and in charge of things, although no one really knows what. I felt at home as soon as I walked through the doors of the BBC.

Anyway, the point is that both versions of what I assumed to be middle age just looked terrific in their own ways. If you can't see it, you can't be it – but I could see it and I was expecting to be very happy being it.

I am now fifty-three. And how do I find middle age?

Well. Surprise, surprise, it's not quite as advertised.

Shall we make some helpful lists for comparison? It's the kind of thing that you do in your fifties:

Things that have remained the same:

1. Dodgy roofers on the prowl
2. Rich men swinging their pants
3. Women feeling vulnerable
4. Male prejudice being fought against
5. Middle-aged people drinking too much.

Things that have changed:

1. The way we look (jumpsuit and trainers anyone?)
2. Our desire to be middle-aged
3. Our acceptance of it when we get there
4. Er . . . when middle age even is
5. Women can now eat Yorkie bars, mainly because the truckers have their hands full with all the Brexit paperwork.

Where's the shoe-mending and pootling around gone? I can't see that version of jumper-clad middle age any more. It's not in my peripheral view. Not in my meta-phorical one either. And certainly not in my direct line of sight, which is Hackney in East London. Cities, in this country at least, don't hold on to their older people very well. I'm not too surprised by that. Just the way of life; the lack of community, the cost and the pace are enough to put people off staying if they have a choice to leave. As proof of that, let's shimmy up to some statistics and ask them to dance? There are nearly three times as many thirty-two-year-olds living in Hackney as there are fifty-two-year-olds, and there are more thirty-two-year-olds here than the entire community of over-eighty-fives. Compare that to Shropshire, where you'll see as many seventy-one-year-olds as fifty-one-year-olds, while just 10 per cent of its population are in their twenties.

You may well be reading this in a part of the country that has, like Shropshire, a more even human distribution, in which case do send your sympathies to a borough where youth trumps age and just imagine all of the businesses that creates, the sheer speed of people on the pavements and the lack of sensible handrails.

There are other things at play here. I also had my kids relatively late in life, a trend the world over. I was thirty-six when I had my son and nearly forty when I popped my daughter out. There is a lot to be said for being an older mum – perhaps the simple knowledge that everything passes, so just take a very deep breath and press on. But the downside is that it reminds you on a daily basis just how achingly, head-bangingly tired and old you already are when you are doing something that in a way keeps you quite young.

And the final nail in the coffin – a turn of phrase for which I offer you no apologies at all – is the youthquake of the industry I work in. Not just the BBC, which has to place a very heavy emphasis on youth because otherwise it is going to slide off a cliff with its ageing audience – an argument I understand but also struggle with. I like to discuss this struggle with my dog and two cats most nights because my kids are busy on Netflix, Snapchat or TikTok.

The gist of the argument my pets patiently sit through is that we might be doing our kids an immense disservice if we pander to their world *too* much. I totally understand market forces, and I appreciate that all of the most exciting things in the world are either created by or for people younger than me, but surely you also need to know about the stuff that lies ahead. There's no point in having a sat nav if you can't key in the destination. Wouldn't it be better to try to stay in it all together?

Is it possible that, if there had been a few more older voices in the room when some of the planet-bending new tech companies were burgeoning, we might not be in quite such a mess? I like to think that a couple of wise but grumpy middle-aged mums might have been able to see that vulnerable, eager-to-please young people all comparing their lives with each other – and being bombarded with a constant popularity contest of ticks and likes before we even get to unchecked male libidos – well, that might end in something quite unpleasant.

I also don't know anyone who can afford to slow down in what now passes for middle age. We still have so much ahead of us – kids who might need funds for further education, parents who are living longer and needing higher levels of care. Mortgages that won't be paid off for years. I will be too old to do much with a pension by the time I can afford to take one. I am not resenting this – how fabulous it all is – but I feel I am on the same conveyor belt going at the same speed as I did twenty years ago. There will simply be no pootling allowed.

If our version of middle age has been chased down by the hounds of youth, it's also being eyed up by the vultures of old age.

In this same borough of youth where I live, there is a new development of flats just by London Fields. It looks nice. The apartments have balconies and there's a bit in the middle with some plants, which you just know was described in the brochure as a 'vibrant communal garden'. From the flats at the top you'd look out over the Fields with their rustling trees. Lovely. But it's not for everyone. It's only for older people. And older people with a lot of cash. It's one step down from sheltered housing – it is a 'retirement community'. And you have to be over fifty-five to get in. Yup, I know . . . *over fifty-five*. So I could in two years' time *move into a retirement community*. It's very confusing. It's tempting to apply just to see what would happen when I explain that when I get to fifty-five, I'll still have seventeen years on the mortgage and two teens living with me at home. They can't want them vaping in the 'vibrant communal garden'.

What does *this* bit of the puzzle mean? Is our generation about to skip middle age altogether and jump straight to old age? Does it matter if we do? I'm not hating where I am now. I like my fifties. A lot. I absolutely totally do. Bigger things come into play than what someone thinks of your puffball. Relationships make more sense. Both the ones that work and the ones that don't. There's a kind of bravery I wasn't expecting; it doesn't come from doing stuff, it comes from not doing it.

And you can just be more honest. Mexican food – yes. A night out at the theatre – no. Staying in mid-range hotels – yes. Staying in a friend's spare room – no.

So if we are to jump straight from young to old, what exactly are we looking at when we're 'old'? As the young people would say, 'the optics' are not good.

Recently, throughout the pandemic, the way we have talked about old people has said so much about where they are in our society. We have largely talked *about* them, not *to* them. We have not really *heard* from them, even though those minds contain so much of the wisdom that might see us through this painful time. Many are old enough to remember a childhood during the Second World War with its curfews and lack of continuous schooling and evacuation and tragedy. They have lessons about love and loss and grief and surviving that we need to hear. Most people who have lived a long life will have some pearls of wisdom that might help to see us through. But are we listening to these stories, or are we only talking about old people as a difficult thing – most likely to die from Covid, needing to be sealed away, *kept alive*, then looked at from a distance?

Even before Covid, our image of old age in this country seemed to veer towards unappealing. From advertising alone you could be forgiven for thinking the third age is mainly about falling over and avoiding the danger posed by water. Walk-in baths, sit-down showers, handrails a-go-go. Combine that with all the terror of slipping – anti-slip bathmats, shoes with extra grip – I'm amazed cruises are so popular.

A wonderful woman called Joan sent an email to us at the *Listening Project* HQ a couple of months back saying all of this. Joan is in her nineties and she said she was really fed up with never hearing or seeing herself reflected on TV and radio talking about normal things.

Life, clothes, food, politics, relationships – just stuff. She's right: when was the last time you heard from an old person as a person, not just as old? The *Project* paired her up with Joyce – a couple of years younger at eighty-six – and of course the result was just wonderful. They talked about all kinds of things. Found lots in common. So many people got back to us to say, 'Brilliant – how rare to hear the J and Js of this world', adding the classic radio accolade – 'Give 'em a show of their own.' I really wish someone would.

Perhaps you don't need role models at the age of fifty-three. I think it turns out that I do. Even if the middle age I imagined lay ahead of me has turned out to be nothing like it in reality, at least a vision of it was there. I can count on the fingers of one hand the number of women over seventy on TV. And I'm not even going to bother counting the 'won't make it to week three' ones on *Strictly*/*I'm a Celeb*/*Prancing on Ice*. When Angela Rippon and Joan Bakewell retire we are left with Prue Leith, Miriam Margolyes and er . . . are you scrabbling around, too? It's quite poor isn't it? We can't leave it all to Brenda Blethyn with an occasional guest appearance from Judi Dench. But just imagine if you popped those women round a table and pressed record. What is it that we are so afraid we'll see and hear? I'm pretty sure you'd get wisdom, humour, experience, candour, hope, filth and everything in between. So why isn't it there?

And yes, in case you are wondering, I do intend to leave a draft copy of this chapter on a bean bag just outside the

Frankie Howerd meeting room in Broadcasting House in the hope that BBC commissioners read it. I have other remarkable programme ideas* about, and for, and with old people, not just these, you know.

Apart from anything else, I need to work for the next, er . . . forty years please.

JANE

I'D LOVE TO THINK BBC COMMISSIONERS are reading this, Fi, but I think we know they're not. Caspian's probably busy at a skateboard park. Dulcie will be with her shaman. Bitter? Me? Certainly not.

Memo to self: do not become one of 'those'. The old stager who pushes off, then makes a good living writing articles, all of which could be called 'It Was Better In My Day'. I will not be that person; unless I become really desperate.

Still, Fi's right – our industry does have a thing about youth. The BBC can sometimes seem like the institutional equivalent of the late-thirties male on the motorised scooter. Mate, people are laughing at you.

Young people are brilliant – they know and understand loads of things I don't. Middle-aged people have already been young, and know how much they knew at twenty-two compared to how much they know now. We

---

* One other idea, quite average and possibly done before on ITV3.

must therefore extend that same courtesy to our elders, who surely despair at our idiocy.

I'm not sure I looked forward to middle age exactly, but then I'm not the sort of person who actively looks forward to much, at least not publicly. Which is one of many reasons why I'm pretty good at being middle-aged. I certainly wasn't best suited to youth, which involved endless energy-sapping activities such as going out and enjoying myself. I really did spend time in the toilet at teenage parties reading *Down and Out in Paris and London*. They didn't call me 'Chuckles' for nothing.

Fi always sounds like she did youth rather well, and therefore deserves to cruise calmer waters with her silver fox, who's a light social drinker with no hint of facial blotching. Once the mortgage is paid off. Which will be about 2054. Let's hope she doesn't wind up on one of those Norovirus hell trips. I'm sure she won't. Though they do seem quite common, don't they?

To think I once enjoyed disparaging the middle-aged and the delight they took in their mundane lives. I obviously had to go through the motions in my youth, pretending I really, really wanted to go on the Magic Bus to Morocco, but there was this essay I had to be getting on with. If only I had the time, but my expert analysis of Philip Sidney's *Astrophel and Stella* waits for no bus with dodgy air-conditioning!

My dad once brought great joy to my sister and me by going to a new municipal tip and enjoying the experience so much he sought out the bloke in charge to tell him what a well-run establishment it was. That was fine, but then he made the mistake of telling the wider family: 'I said to the chap, I said, what a wonderful, well-run tip you've got here.' We were beside ourselves. And no, not with admiration for his thoughtfulness.

By the way, if you want to bring your parents great joy, don't bother trying to get an Olympic medal or a literary prize. I know, their grandchildren aside, that I've really delighted mine on just two occasions; once, when I put petrol into a diesel car, causing a magnificent, costly and time-consuming kerfuffle, and recently, when I sat on a chair in a lovely café and it promptly collapsed beneath me. They were eighty-five and eighty-six at the time and laughed like bloody drains. No, I wasn't badly hurt. Just light bruising. Still, it's a good illustration of Fi's point that the 'elderly' (us, soon, and that's if we're lucky) do not all form part of a helpless, cuddly, benign sort of blob. They are not all just sitting around in front of a one-bar electric fire in a foot muff, waiting for something bad to happen. Or for *Pointless* to start. No, they're in rural cafés on the Mersey Riviera choking on their chocolate-covered flapjacks with mirth as their Radio 4 presenter daughter, who lectures them about all manner of things and tells them off for believing everything they read in the papers, lands arse over tit on the floor.

We know youth is all about uncertainty and floundering and trying to fit in. And, yes, desperately caring what other people think about your fringe or your jacket, while maintaining the illusion that you don't give a damn.

That's what youth is for. Unfortunately, I'm able to tell you now that, from my perspective, youth has a lot in common with middle age. If you're an introvert like me, who enjoys reading and making soup, then admittedly it's easier socially, because you're no longer expected to dedicate entire weekends to good times, which can make you feel bad all week (some people in middle age do behave like this, and they're called men, and we now know they're having a midlife crisis).

But. You are still riddled with self-doubt in middle age. Still often only capable of being 'not sure'. Once you worried about spots; now you must be on twenty-four-hour guard for signs of ageing and apply serum accordingly. It's way too late to have potential. By now, I'm afraid, you should have achieved it.

So when does the famed confidence of middle age descend? This is where I think Fi should try to put away her worries about getting old. I am prepared to make the case for old age. I want to believe there's a sweet spot, just before you start – very sensibly – worrying about taking a tumble. You've not hit the age of regularly spouting xenophobic nonsense about foreigners, but you know your own mind. Oh, very much so. Imagine you're walking life's highway, decently shod, all wrapped up, and the sun's out. A stranger bids you good morning, and asks you the way to the post office. You are able to furnish them with this information in good time, and they go on their way. You are a solid citizen. You like what you know; you know what you like.

The next day, sadly, you trip over your exercise bike and it's pretty much downhill from there.

9

OH SHUT UP, ROGER:

ENTITLEMENT, CHINOS AND EYE TESTS

JANE

MAY A HIGHER BEING GRANT me the confidence of a booming man.

You've been patronised by him. You've definitely sat in meetings with him. Or next to him at a dinner party. You've been trapped with him at a conference, by the lunchtime finger buffet; you've got half an eye on the last Mexican bean wrap, just beginning to stiffen at its curvy corners, he's droning on. And on. Someone else comes along and takes it! Damn. You might have to settle for another fistful of crisps. Roger didn't notice you were distracted; he's busily telling you about another time he was right about something.

It's hard to break away when he's in full flow. You've been taught to be polite in these situations, and we all know what happens to pushy women who butt in. Be honest: do you, regularly, enable a Roger in your life? Have you ever been in a position where you have done so? And yes, that does include feeding one on a regular basis. You may well be related to a Roger. In some extreme cases, you may wake up one day to find you are actually married to one. Oh dear.

Actually I saw one the other day, loping along, linen jacket flapping, slap-bang in the middle of the road – no mere pavement for our boy! It was early on a summer's morning, and I was heading off for my steps in the park, doing my little bit to fend off decrepitude. I can't age a Roger exactly, but I'd say this was a pretty typical specimen: a white chap in, possibly, his late fifties. That's a fair few years off his intellectual and reproductive prime, but Roger's still a bit of a hit on the social circuit. No shortage of invites for him. He's probably the ultimate 'spare man'. Now, I know it's not logical or fair to jump to a conclusion about any individual on the basis of their lolloping, entitled stride down the centre of a quiet road first thing in the morning, but I'm afraid logic and fairness play no part in this. Sorry, Roger, you really grind my gears. And I hate linen jackets. Jackets that say, 'I'm too much of an intellectual maverick to wear structured clothing.' But let's leave him to his business. He's bound to have a host of important things to do.

I can talk, obviously. And I'm a fine one to talk about other people talking too much. But it's different for women, for a woman can never be a Roger. Or a change-jiggler, as we used to call them. It's the early 1990s, a summer's afternoon at my first BBC local radio station in Worcester. I was low in the pecking order, a status that I richly deserved. The other very junior reporter was my good friend Lucy, and to some members of staff we appeared more or less interchangeable. Janeorlucy. Lucyorjane. Both small, determined, profoundly irritating. We were allowed out to cover barn fires and giant veg, and occasionally got the chance to read the notoriously insignificant 2 p.m. news bulletin. The afternoon news had none of the obvious glamour of the lunchtime update and wasn't sufficiently close to the evening to have even a hint of primetime about it. Needless to say, I gave it my all. If there'd been a spate of thefts from garden sheds in the Leominster area, I treated it with the gravity it deserved. Or perhaps, rather more than it deserved. Not that anyone wants to lose a good spade, obviously. I'd have worn full evening dress if I could.

Meanwhile, the senior men (yes, they were all men) in the newsroom would gather in a butch clump around the only telly, 'keeping an eye' on the test match. They'd exchange expert views on how things were progressing, while busily jostling their hands around in the deep pockets of their beige High Street slacks. These men were not nasty; sometimes their praise and encouragement could make me blush. But Lucy and I would still be both baffled and infuriated by this manly huddle. How could we ever hope to penetrate this bubble of testosterone? Dare we risk a comment of our own about a wayward full toss? For all our spark and indignation, we dared not. This was still a world of men. And we were jolly lucky to be in it. Now, what was the weight of that marrow?

I know this is hardly El Vino's, the legendary Fleet Street bar that wouldn't even serve women, and I know how much things have changed for the better in the last thirty years in journalism. If you want to find out about the real female pioneers read Julie Welch's book *The Fleet Street Girls*. Contempt, bafflement, slaps on the bum and the indomitable spirit of the women – it's all there.

I'm sure this is a minority interest, but I've long been intrigued by newspaper picture bylines and media publicity shots of men and women. They neatly sum up the way we're allowed to be seen and heard. The women are fully made-up, ultra-buffed versions of themselves, usually smiling. A little winsome. 'Sassy' at a push. There's even an element of the 'Come hither' about some of them. 'Hey, nothing to fear here! I may be a clever old soul and a witty contrarian with something to add to the national debate, but I'd still very much welcome an approach, Roger, old boy.' Sorry – him again. Owning my own hypocrisy here, I feel honour-bound to point out that I'm never happier than when someone uses a ten-year-old publicity shot of me. The one I like the best looks absolutely nothing like me. Much obliged.

The men in these publicity shots, though . . . There are a few cheeky grins, admittedly. But most of the chaps favour the studied thinking face, the one that suggests a little bit of genius is indeed forming just below the surface and could erupt at any time. Stand well back! Then you get the arms folded, I-mean-business stance. Street fighter, me. Came up the hard way (warning – this can mean they didn't go to Oxford.) Then there's quirky man, angular, hint of a wink; and finally the scowling

Grand Inquisitor, all distinguished wrinkles and heaps of hard-earned attitude. No time for any niceties; I shall damn well duff you up. Perhaps we could go for a spot of lunch afterwards?

Every now and again, the chaps in charge contrive to say or do something so astonishingly entitled it takes breath from even the most battle-scarred of us. And surely gives heart to all the other arch-blusterers in town. Yes, I am revisiting the Cummings Eye Test Driving Claim. Not original, I know. And by the time you read this, possibly pretty old. But I sincerely doubt anyone will have said anything quite so stupid since. (I should've known better: Jacob Rees-Mogg has just said some fish are glad to be British.) If you've wisely chosen to file away 2020 in the darkest of all mental recesses, let me give you a brief refresher. Dominic Cummings was a special adviser to British Prime Minister Johnson. Note – 'adviser'. That is, someone chosen for their wise counsel. And by all accounts – and certainly his own – the man has an absolute scorcher of a brain. He could, indeed, see the way the wind was blowing in terms of the European Union; he masterminded the Conservative election victory of December 2019. But then – well, we know what happened then. Mr Cummings helped come up with many of the rules of the first lockdown and was caught out breaking some of them. Stricken by Covid but starting a recovery, and stuck somewhere he really shouldn't have been, he took a drive to see whether it would be safe to drive.

Yes. That's still right. He thought coronavirus may have affected his vision, so he got in a car with his wife and child and went for a drive. AND THEN SAID SO ON NATIONAL TELEVISION.

We need to keep saying how magnificently bloody stupid this statement is. It will never not be utterly ridiculous. As explanations go, it stank like that rotting stub of Stilton you bought for the festive season and found again in late May, just behind the jar of cranberry sauce dating from 2005.

We've all done very stupid, even reckless things. I myself remain that demented woman who spent an entire weekend trying to find the right sprocket to attach a new garden hose to an outside tap and lost a number of friends by dwelling on it. I once asked an eminent historian where Eleanor of Aquitaine was from. I was caught off-mic impersonating a guest on a radio programme I'd just presented – pathetic showing-off in the first degree.

And yes, Cummings's statement was widely mocked at the time. It was the subject of cartoons, hate-filled jibes on social media, wisecracks on panel shows. And yet the man retained a modicum of credibility. Slack, somehow, was cut. People – not just men, by any means – came to his defence. He was 'doing the right thing by his family'. Eh? He clung on to his job for months afterwards, merrily advising away. As I type, the Power Goblin has resurfaced, spitting venom and making claims of foolish and unethical behaviour at the very heart of the government he helped to run. He also said it was 'crackers' that he had the job in the first place. He is being taken very seriously.

I've looked around, and I can see no female equivalent of the Roger. True equality will surely only be achieved when women can be total arseholes in public, too, and other people leap willingly to their defence. Including men. The ambition for a female Roger is a close cousin of my earlier and reasonably successful campaign, Let's Get More Mediocre Women to the Top. It's true that neither slogan would work well on a T-shirt – you can see why my career as an advertising copywriter didn't pan out. But look, my intentions are good. I just want women to feel they too can speak up, speak out, and routinely bore the pants off other people in public. And you don't have to be right, or clever. Do remember that.

You may listen to more radio than me, but I doubt it. I never feel more alone than in the endless conversations about the television box-set binge everyone else is on. I am quite immune to series with subtitles about Belgian undertakers/Swedish architects/Brazilian counter-intelligence operations. No, I don't really love the interiors in that show about the Spanish drug-runner and her pet donkey. (I don't count my *Inside the World's Toughest Prisons* habit – that's between my therapist and me.) Generally speaking, while you're busily working your way through series seven ('What do you think? Could you do one more before bed?'), I'm listening to talk radio in the bath, cogitating in the healing waters. Yes, I do sometimes use those post-workout bath salts without having done a workout. It's not a crime. Anyway, here I am exposed to much wisdom. Here, men with a view roam free, untamed – though not necessarily un-challenged, I should say.

They have a LOT to say, these chatty men on talk radio. And they are wonderfully unencumbered by self-doubt. The sort of self-doubt that might, perhaps, make you think twice about calling in. They all suffer from the exact opposite of Imposter Syndrome, and I don't think there's a cure for it. It does remind me of my adolescence and the quite brilliant lunchtime phone-in on BBC Radio Merseyside, when callers from all corners of the region – how we love a region – would be offered a chance to express a view on current affairs. It's one of the area's many strengths that neither sex truly needs much encouragement to say what they think, but even here men tended to dominate. Trouble in the Middle East? Yes, Ron in Tuebrook may well have a hot take. Eat your heart out, Madeleine Albright. Economy tanking? Bring in Derek from Knotty Ash. He works part-time in a bookie's. Give that man the keys to No. 11 right now.

Fast-forward forty years, and Rogers still abound on all these shows. The complexities of Brexit were cer-tainly no match for them. Minutes after the withdrawal agreement was published in 2018, they were hogging the airwaves again, all necessary detail absorbed. Speedy readers, these blokes. Let's go to Barry in Dagenham, he's not a fan: and on he goes, expertly pulling the agreement apart, analysing its flaws, finding it severely wanting.

Play Brexit Bingo: sovereignty, Northern Irish backstops, fishing rights, protecting our borders, chuck in another mention of sovereignty towards the end. Thousands of pages, hours of time, bundles of taxpayers' money, all those great brains on both sides. Why on earth didn't we just get Barry to sort it all out? He's not busy on Wednesdays.

Trust me: on Brexit phone-ins, women were rarer than hen's teeth. Why? Well sometimes the only reasonable or logical response to a complex issue is 'I don't know' – and I acknowledge that doesn't make compelling radio. Where would we listeners be without good old Barry? Still, let's take a moment to consider the power of the clever man who sometimes says he doesn't know – it's one of the things that makes Britain's Deputy Chief Medical Officer, Jonathan Van-Tam, such a brilliant and effective communicator. There are levels of clever that simply don't require any bullshit. And it's very, very attractive. I once met a man who was so high up in top-secret stuff it would make all your pips squeak, but he carried himself like a thoroughly decent geography teacher, the sort of person you'd really trust to get your daughter through her GCSE. If you're the real thing, you don't need to bother pretending. Heavy sigh. Enough about him.

Which brings me to the many, many women I have met and interviewed, and their apparent reluctance to embrace their natural brilliance. So frustrating, and yet so easy to understand. Lacking the entitlement of a Roger, we want to be liked, but we don't assume we will be; we certainly don't assume it's our right. Self-deprecation done well can be part of a winning formula, but don't overdo it. Honestly, I was well into my forties before I realised that taking yourself seriously can lead to other people taking you seriously, too. I feel a fool for not understanding that sooner. And that's not self-deprecation, it's the truth.

At 9.30 a.m. the *Woman's Hour* green room at Broadcasting House would often be positively fizzing with brilliant, clever, talented women. I loved going in before the programme to chat to the day's guests – it felt the polite thing to do, but it was also very good fun. Unlikely alliances were formed, useful connections made. The programme's madly diverse brief (basically, 'women') meant you could easily find an up-and-coming star of British grime, an emeritus professor of microbiology, a trade-union leader and a tech entrepreneur all sharing the same small space, swapping email addresses and politely indulging my terrible small talk. (The Garvey small talk: to anyone British, weak gag about the lousy BBC hospitality being limited to a range of herbal and traditional tea, strictly no biscuits; to anyone from abroad, 'Are you in London long?' Never fails.)

Most guests were happy to meet me and chat through some of the things I might ask. Many were, of course, competent, highly intelligent people who could happily have dealt with my probing in their sleep. But a number of women would ask me, slightly nervously, if it would be 'all right' if they brought their notes into the studio with them, the notes they had just delved into their cavernous bag to find, to flick through for reassurance one more time. Sometimes, I realised, they were so uncertain of themselves that the experience would be much easier for them if they had their notes in their hand. They wouldn't need them, not for a minute, but what the hell. Occasionally, though, I would find myself becoming terribly firm and simply telling a woman in no uncertain terms that she was at the top of her bloody game, an expert in her field, multi-award-winning . . . and no, she really wouldn't need those precious notes in her lap in order to be interviewed by me (I nearly said little old me there, but I'm learning).

I'm not remotely surprised the women asked, not really. I understood it. And actually I liked them for it. Some were a similar age to me, doing constant battle with the self-doubt that descends in your mid-forties, hovering over your working day, picking away at your ability to make any decisions or any sense. About the same time, in fact, that you acquire that cavernous handbag you can't find anything in. Apart from used tissues. You can always find them.

And what about the women who swanned in, cool as you like, entirely unperturbed and more than eager to lend us their genius? Oh, I was never as keen on them. Bit full of themselves, if you ask me.

Anyway, if you're reading this, Roger – give us a call sometime.

FI

MEXICAN BEAN WRAP, YOU SAY? Is that wise ahead of a long afternoon in an airless conference room?

I hear your frustrations and I sympathise with them. On a macro scale, you could legitimately blame most of the ills of the current modern world on men who've been allowed to roam free too much. On the micro level, let's start with Roger's linen, which makes no sense either. Such an unforgiving fabric. One crease and it looks sack-like. One drop of perspiration and it looks soaked. And where is the structure, Jane, where is the support?

Of course, you are also right that these particular men seem to need very little support. Oh, actually, hang on a sec, is support via the means of unparalleled attention what they are actually after? OMG look at that – only ten seconds into 'having a point of view about something' and I am questioning my own judgement.

I'd like Roger to shut up, too. Not just so we could hear more from the female audience, but also to make way for the beta male. His is a voice I'd like to hear much more of. I'd like to hear the beta male telling the alpha male to pipe down. I'd like the beta male to be the go-to role model for your average young man. By 'beta male' I mean a bloke who doesn't have to win at any cost, can find happiness in the success or contentment of others and hasn't limited his only sincere experience of decent female love, irrespective of his sexuality, to that which he has for his mum. The problem is that it is very hard to celebrate the type of person whose very appeal is that they don't clamour to be celebrated.

The beta male quite possibly also understands how conversation works. Which is important, because quite a bit of this is played out in our tiny world of radio. I'm not surprised women are fearful of their own expertise suddenly disappearing when the mic comes on – because what you hear all around you has not been very encouraging. It really is still a thing – men talking over women. You hear women trying, very nicely at first and then with increasing annoyance, to just get a word in edgeways. I wonder what these men think the expression on the face of their interviewer or audience means. Is there just a whole chart of human understanding that they haven't seen? One where the person in front of them is going boss-eyed with boredom or puce with frustration – and they, as if colour-blind and swearing that red is green, think, 'Oh yes, that means this is going down jolly well'?

I sense that you have reached a point of no return in facilitating Rogers. I think thirteen years at the helm of the SS *Woman's Hour* would be enough to dampen the spirits of even the most upbeat facilitating woman.

You must wonder what else exactly it is that we women have to do if we have already fought the battles, died at the races, been imprisoned, been released, relit the brazier, introduced the 10.45 p.m. 'drama' quite professionally – and then done it all again. Women have shouted and asked nicely. Women have written books about how equality is enshrined in law. Written manuals about how to get through the barricades at work. How to do it obviously. Even how to do it slyly. We have made spreadsheets about how women can make companies more money.

But yes, maybe we've been missing the obvious – why haven't we just aped the really appalling male behaviour that seems almost expected of you, and is certainly forgiven, when you reach the very top? Why haven't women had more kiddies with their lovers, made more dubious investments to line their own pockets, clung on to their jobs with the 'full backing' of their bosses, even though other people lost theirs as a result. There's that super-confidence again – 'full backing'. Not 'well – I can see both sides' backing.

And so to your point about Dominic Cummings.

What struck me so much about that piece of political posturing was that we witnessed lines being crossed in such plain sight. The double standards weren't acted upon in so very many ways. He said he'd got in a car and driven, to see if he could see. Did the DVLA call him up and take away his licence? Did his car insurers negate his policy – using the 'what a total prat' clause? Did social services mark his card about his parenting skills? Nope. None of that. The distant warning bells of logic seemed to be ignored or drowned out by the din created by simply being in a position of power.

The double standard of letting a Roger loose has more sinister effects. Unchecked men cost women their lives.

I'm writing this in the week of Phil Spector's death. A man with a history of weirdness towards women. A man who liked playing with guns. But a man who was very successful at work. Years ago, he told an interviewer that his demons often overtook him. Nothing happened. Hundreds of people in recording studios and record companies witnessed his simmering danger first-hand. And still the records kept on coming. So when Lana Clarkson met him in a nightclub in Los Angeles, how could she possibly have known what was about to happen to her? What she saw was a free and successful man. Society condoned his behaviour by still allowing him that freedom and success. And so she went home with him and became another woman whose life was taken away from her and her family by a man who should have been called out and stopped years before.

But let's not ignore the absolute fact that the constraints within which we have led our female lives are changing. There's a fabulous moment at the end of *Miss Americana*, the documentary about Taylor Swift, where she goes off on one about how she has been treated by the media – and she really lets rip. She then immediately apologises for being so loud. And *then* she catches herself and says, 'Why did I do that? Why am I apologising for being loud in *my own house*, which I bought with the money *I* made from the songs that *I* wrote about the stories in *my own life*?'

She is one of the most powerful young women on the planet. In that moment she said something so many of us have felt. That we don't sit easily in our space. That *we* can never be loud. I liked her so much for calling that out, and it struck me that our salvation might lie in our ability to notice these things in the first place.

I banked that scene. I suspect that Taylor will be in charge of most things by the time she is forty. And she won't have to work with a Phil, or be under the government of a Trump, or put up with a Roger. She has developed a political voice, against all the advice from older managers and advisers that it simply isn't the done thing for a young female country crossover artist to get involved in the big issues of life. Not for her the silencing of the distant bells of logic. Her fate is not that of other female artists who trod the same path before.

And it is possible that Roger may well meet his natural fate, too. If the pavement is indeed just too confining and conforming for him, well . . . here's a thought to end on. Although he can probably hear you grinding your gears from afar while he's sauntering along in the middle of the road, and although that might alert him to the fact that his position as a dominant man might be about to be called in by equally dominant women – it's actually the bloke doing the Covid eye test while driving a car that he needs to watch out for. Foolish men might end up bringing the whole male posturing caboodle down. Roger on Roger action. Copy that.

10

THE FETISHISATION OF DOMESTICITY:

CASHING IN ON MAKING CHORES LOOK NICE

FI

AN ENTRY IN *WHO'S WHO* provides any self-regarding nobody who has become a tiny self-regarding somebody with the wonderful opportunity to commit themselves to history in whatever shape or form they like. It's remarkable that these tomes are still in business, given the power of Google and the ease of Wikipedia. Both of these provide a more critical sense of a person, with more of a 360-degree appraisal, whereas *Who's Who* still gives you a form you can fill in yourself. It's the TripAdvisor of the ego – write your own review, say what you like, someone might check the stuff about school and jobs, but you are also given the chance to tell the world about your hobbies and pastimes, and how is anyone going to verify what you put under 'recreations'? Especially when there are entries like 'dreaming on a star' and 'beard maintenance' and 'witchcraft and Venn diagrams'.

The only time I got sent an invitation to join in the fun was in 2006, when I'd just had a baby and had also just gone back to work. I decided to be honest. In fact, I didn't really decide to be honest. This honesty was forced on me. I had no time for hobbies. I was mainly wiping things – a baby's bottom or a mucky surface, or the memories of two decades of what turned out to have been relatively hedonistic, independent fun without leaking nipples. So my recreations are given as 'Domesticity and listening to radio', because those were genuinely the only two things I was doing. A couple of years later, someone picked up on this and gave me a hard time about letting down the sisterhood in admitting to the drudge, they seemed to be suggesting that I was trying in some way to turn back time to about 1954, when 'being house-proud' was a thing that was taught in schools – only to girls, mind you. The boys did woodwork or were asked to write essays with titles like 'Are you a lover or a fighter? Discuss in no more than 500 words. Use examples of your own experience where necessary.'

But should I feel bad about something that sometimes makes me feel good?

I wasn't trying to paint myself in a sepia tint of housewifery for *Who's Who* readers, nor was I trying to score some kind of ironic political point. It was true that 'domesticity' was where I was spending most of my time. It is for most of us in those days of parenting young children, and when I say most I mean mostly women. I can pretty much guarantee that there isn't a single entry in *Who's Who* by a man citing his recreations as 'dusting, hoovering and swathes of overwhelming laundry'. And often it is overwhelming. I have looked on with envy at those who have genuinely shared heavy lifting/scouring/hoovering responsibilities with their partners. I know of one couple who take it in turns to do a month of the laundry, and I regard them both with the kind of wonder other people might affect if in the presence of a Beatle or an Obama. I'm now raising a son and a daughter, and one of my most sincere hopes is that the next generation of men don't even have to think before loading a machine or cleaning a surface or – your favourite, I know, Jane – pulling hair out of a plughole. There will be no special badge of honour or pat on the back from a mother-in-law who says, 'Oh look he changed a nappy! How lucky you are to have him, dear!' Of course he should change a nappy. Without applause.

But I suspect that until there is a Mr Hinch, this might not be so easy. It annoys and surprises me that there hasn't yet been a Mr Hinch. Actually, there is a real-life one who is married to Mrs Hinch, but he hasn't made a mint out of being domestic, and none of this makes sense if you don't know who Mrs Hinch is. And in case you don't know, I'll fill you in. She is the thirty-year-old domestic goddess of cleaning who has made a small fortune out of her cleaning tips. Full name Sophie Hinchliffe, she is married to sales exec Jamie Hinchliffe, they have a son Ronnie and, at the time of writing, another on the way. She is an admirable grafter, and has been since leaving school. After any number of waitressing/low-paid/long-hours jobs she trained to be a hairdresser before she started putting her household cleaning tips – along with pics of her immaculate house in Maldon, Essex – up on Instagram, and the rest is a short and lucrative ride across the modern horizon of likes and shares and branded content; and she's been on Steve Wright in the afternoon. Mrs Hinch is now a multi-bestselling author, blogger and Insta sensation with over 4 million followers. She is described on her Wiki page as a 'cleaning influencer'. Quite a job title. And her house – and how she cleans it – is something to behold.

It is highly addictive domestic porn. By this I don't mean 'Knock knock. Oh look, it's the plumber and I've not had time to get dressed . . .' I mean it embodies a current fetishisation of house-cleaning and chores. What a time to be human, when you can scroll through page after page of unachievable cleanliness and consider whether or not you should buy a pair of 'mop slippers', which are exactly what you think they are – slippers with mops on the bottom so you can glide round your house cleaning the floor with your feet as you go. I want them. I want them now (£8.99 on eBay, in case you are wondering).

Yet we've always liked to look inside people's houses. I imagine there was a time when it was even interesting to see how other cave dwellers kept their surroundings. Pamela would pop back from a quick visit to the trog-lodytes down the road on the pretext of offering them some of their leftover boar-chunk-on-a-stick, only to return with woodpile envy: 'Derek you'd never believe what they've done with their kindling!'

As a child I was happiest in the back of the car when we drove through towns and suburbs just so that I could take a quick peek in the windows of everyone else's homes – tiny vistas of other styles, other ways of living, whole lives displayed in sofa choices and curtains and frosted-glass porches.

As a grown up I haven't changed all that much. I just find myself more conflicted. That's a word you never have to use as a child when you are still allowed to be completely certain about everything in the moment but nothing for any length of time. Who doesn't mourn a time in their life when they could tell Susie they loved Jamie on a Monday but by Wednesday liked Eddie and not tell Susie and by Friday were totally into skateboarding so who cares?

It's annoying that the adult world is more complex. I always wanted to go out to work, and a lot of the appeal of that was simply to be out of the house most of the day. As a younger woman I had no ambition to get married and 'stay home', but I don't dismiss it as the easy option, or an old-fashioned one, or some kind of entrapment of the female form – as long as it has been your choice and you have found fulfilment in it, then I salute you. Some days it must be easier than the endless fight for a place in the working world and too many Tube journeys spent in someone's armpit considering if this was what you got that degree for. Some days I bet it's not. It's also not a given that if you choose to stay home you must clean all day. Watch K-pop if you want to, swing from a filthy chandelier – I'm not judging you as long as you aren't judging me in return.

There has always been plenty of literature to support the domestic choice, particularly in the form of magazines. The newsagent's stand doesn't seem to have moved along with the times as much as the audience standing in front of it. From *Take a Break* to *Good Housekeeping*, you can always find a decent recipe for a midweek shepherd's pie or a tip for cleaning the grout far more easily than you can get a magazine that helps you navigate the workplace or tells you how to fill in your tax return. Where is *Good HMRC Bookkeeping* when we need it?

Mrs Beeton has a lot to answer for. Her success set something of a commercial one. Her *Book of Household Management* was actually a compilation of recipes she had originally collected for the sexily entitled Englishwoman's Domestic Magazine, owned by her publisher husband Samuel. Most came from readers and were not even her own, but the idea to bundle up these twenty-four instalments into a book was the Beetons' – and I do hope they offered a free binder with Part One.

For the huge impact she has had in the domestic arena of our lives, Mrs Beeton's own was short-lived and filled with sadness. She lost her father at the age of four and was sent to a German boarding school, while her mother remarried and went on to have thirteen children. Beeton herself lost two children in infancy and died from a fever after the birth of her son. She was only twenty-eight. To have worked as she did through all of that, to compile and complete what was described as the publishing sensation of its era – *Household Management* sold 60,000 copies in its first year alone – well, I'm doffing my hat to you, Isabella.

And it was regarded at the time as a liberating force – encouraging women to enjoy the dark arts of pastry, with added sections on poisons and how to keep your pantry regime tight. Almost all any life needs. It also brought women together (that's just the burgeoning middle-class variety of women) with a book that was about their day-to-day lives. She was exploited after her death, with the publishers pretending that she was still alive, or at least not exactly recognising that she was dead, in order to maintain sales of *Household Management*. I know. I winced, too. There is so much money to be made behind the veneer of domestic satisfaction, who cares about the actual truth?

And the truth is that you need to polish it and fetishise it. No one wants to watch or read about someone actually mopping a floor or stirring porridge, or spending the whole of Tuesday putting wet sheets through a mangle so of course it has to be jazzed up in order to sell, and the more places there are to sell, the more jazzed up the domestic needs to be. Take a leap of 100 years; no modern woman has better understood that than Martha Stewart. The picture-perfect high-end Americana domesticity in her magazines and TV shows has created a multimillion-dollar business courtesy of moppets muppets like me. I'll confess to hours of daydreaming pleasure and a fantastic facial workout (eyebrows up, everyone! And again! And again!) reading features about her understairs storage solutions, her pumpkin patches and her clever ideas for celebrating Labor Day using only a pack of parchment paper, some blue velvet ribbons and three fresh avocados.

Martha often uses her own homes as illustrations for inspiration, and so she shows us around her Map Room – yes, it does what it says on the tin, it's a room just for your maps and if you want to make a joke about not being able to find it you're on your own there. You'll find handy pieces about how to turn small, cramped areas of your home into present-wrapping stations, too. I want to condemn her for this, but actually I'd love one. It's like trying to put the Hadron Collider together in our house when someone needs wrapping paper, scissors and Sello-tape all at the same time. Try to find some ribbon too and you can hear the cries in space

For me it doesn't stop with Martha. You might be familiar with the very neat work of Marie Kondo and her clear-out-your-cupboards-and-clear-out-your soul message. I certainly am. I once sat through a whole half-hour of Anthea Turner on TV showing me how to fold shirts and jumpers properly. On being told this anecdote, a friend offered to stage an intervention if it ever happened again.

All these domesticity multimillionaires tap into our desire to take a bath in domestic perfection, even if our own is a bit scummy around the top. And so Mrs

Hinch is just the latest celebrant. Where Martha does clever things with teal and burnt-amber soft-furnishing combos, Sophie's home is described as being a 'calming palette of white and grey'. It looks a little bit like you are watching black and white TV. She is fond of an ornate mirror and those wordy things on walls:

Dance like no one is watching!
Love like you've never been hurt!
Paint something on a wall that makes you
sound nice!

Although Mrs Hinch presents an uncluttered vision of her world, her cleaning cupboard is stuffed to the gunnels with products. Bleaches, scrubs, stain-removing mousses and powders and potions and sprays. Kerching. The brand management is busy.

I enjoy nosing around in Mrs Hinch's world, not because I want my house to look like that but because I know it can't. My childhood aspirations came good and I now 'work outside the home', as George W. Bush learned to say in order not to offend the massively important American Mom demographic. So I have done a day's work by the time I come back to my 'at home' shift. And, yes, I do have a cleaner, too. Three hours a week.

So what's the niggle? Why am I even bothering to tell you all this? Women making their own money out of something that all of us have to do can only be a good thing. Looking at nice pictures of other people's houses is hardly a crime. Aspiring to live a more domestically creative life isn't everyone's cup of tea, neither is it a front-page story. The niggle is that, despite all the pornification of plumping a cushion or scouring a surface and the occasional massive fortune amassed in recent times – we still haven't solved the problem of the domestic being regarded as 'women's work'. In fact, it's not regarded as women's work – it just is women's work. Statistics show that most domestic chores are still undertaken by women. The most recent National Office of Statistics survey (2016) found that women were still doing a whopping 60 per cent more of the unpaid work in the home than men. Sixty per cent. Not just a tad more than. Not even a bit more than. MORE THAN HALF AGAIN.

So we've done what clever women always do – we've made a silk purse out of a sow's ear. We turned boringly repetitive, dull work into something that is vaguely more enjoyable – or at least we have convincingly told ourselves that it is. We've done this because those chores still need to get done. And guess what – it's left us still having to do them.

Yet where there's money there are usually men. If what it takes for more men to share the load is a simple golden carrot of cash on the end of a stick then could you just get a crack on? Get yourselves some billionaire household-chore role models. Set up an online shop – own your domestic shit, rebrand Marigolds as 'macho grips' if you're struggling with the old-fashioned connotations of 'women's work' – do whatever you like really, but do it soon. There must be a neat and tidy young gent somewhere who'd like to turn his hand to fetishising the domestic for the modern man. Who wouldn't watch an episode of Greg James's Tidy Pantry or live-stream Joe Wicks Works Wonders on Your Grout? Is Jon Snow not free for something more home-based these days?

I'm writing this during the third lockdown of the pandemic, when the bar for every kind of accomplishment has been low. And if all I manage is some tidy pants, I'll take that most days. But here's the honest truth – I am sometimes at my calmest in my tiny laundry cupboard. Mainly because it is a place of quiet. It's away from my other work. Away from the kids. I can do a task from start to finish and relish a tiny moment of satisfaction in an otherwise complicated old world. I am well aware of the fact that I like it because I don't have to do it all the time, and because clever women have enabled me to find something fanciful and escapist about some of it. I am grateful to them for that, even if it's delusional. But would I say the same thing again if asked for my recreations and pastimes? Nah – I'd just make something up to appear glamorous and decadent and oh so very very clever and it'd definitely be something doesn't get me into any kind of trouble. I don't know what though – looking at clouds? Learning the trapeze? Getting ticky about men?

By the way, I don't think I am in *Who's Who* any more. I'm waiting for the form from Who Was She. Any day now, I'm sure.

JANE

I SENSE FI'S LOOKING for a little reassurance here. So just to say you're still very relevant and important. OK?

Moving on – I didn't know Fi during her TWO decades of 'selfish, hedonistic, independent fun'. Just as well. Or did I first encounter her at the fag end of the second decade? Possibly. No wonder she gets her kicks out of feather dusters and a stiff brush these days. She must be exhausted.

And secondly – yes, I have a cleaner, too. Every Tuesday. No feeling like it – returning to a home someone else has tidied for you. Your mess; someone else's responsibility. It's perfect. For a few hours, the place has reached its full potential. I'm not incapable; I'll wipe down and brush up with the best of them, but I'm no pro. I do, though, always have a good go at the toilet before anyone else has to. This is one of the reasons I was so incensed by the Phantom Crapper of Broadcasting House, the deeply flawed (in the absence of anything else publishable, let's settle for that description) individual who would make merry in one of the toilets on the fifth floor, *sans* flush. My home-made pink-highlighter sign 'Do You Behave Like This At Home?' was swiftly taken down by the top-secret organisation BBC Workplace on the grounds that it didn't constitute official signage. That battle is not over, let me tell you. Interestingly, the Crapper wasn't a key worker because there were no incidents during the pandemic. I'll let you know how this one develops. Possibly an ITV three-parter spread over three nights?

I think there's a fair chance male writers wouldn't consider the subject of cleaning at all. Or if they did, they wouldn't think of it as in any way controversial. I very much doubt they would have any hesitation about 'admitting' to having a cleaner. Some probably don't know whether they have one or not. Imagine if, by law, every single book by a man had to begin with an acknowledgement that if they hadn't had someone around to fluff up their cushions and put a stiff crease in their old-man denim, none of their great works could have been written. Didn't the inventor of free trade, Adam Smith, famously live with his mother? He was upstairs loftily coming up with capitalism; his dear old mum was down below cutting the crusts off his sandwiches.

I tell you what, I may have left *Woman's Hour*, but it will sure as hell never leave me. The flame of female indignation burns bright. And that's a good thing, by the way. At the BBC I met the impossibly glamorous Mrs Hinch and, on her recommendation, invested in some floral-scented disinfectant. The stuff she applies to all surfaces before she retires to her boudoir at night. What can I say? I had been well and truly Influenced. And I must say, it mingles wonderfully with eau de cat litter and the insistent pong of too many veggie curries.

I lost count of the number of very important *Woman's Hour* discussions we had on the challenging lives of modern women – now free as birds to work, both inside and outside the home, but usually both. It was clear we were all most assuredly 'up against it'. OK, we may not be dying in childbirth having our eighth child, but you try making Book Club after a hard day at a tech start-up and a tussle with a malfunctioning dishwasher. Occasionally, I'd be forced to confront my own historic hypocrisy. I could see my mother – it's just after 5.30 p.m., she's back from work 'outside the home'; in one swift movement she's acknowledged the dog, dumped a bag on the counter and she's already in the fridge, footling for all the ingredients for her much-needed drink. Gearing up for her next shift, which I can now tell her is called 'invisible labour'. And then she's confronted by a teenage arse like me, who reminds her she hates corned-beef hash and why doesn't she ever remember?

I wasn't thoughtful; I didn't notice; there's no excuse. It's curious that someone who takes a certain amount of pride in her ability to empathise professionally could behave in this way, but maybe we grow into empathy – or maybe we never see the need to employ it in our 'real' life.

I should say I totally commend Fi's attempts to bring up her daughter and her son in the same way, expecting them both to do their domestic bit. As I have been blessed with two daughters, I do not have this issue. We've settled the matter entirely here by letting me do everything, and it works like a dream. After every meal, as they prepare to scarper, I attempt the same weak joke: 'Oh, is it my turn to clear up?' And it is! And I do it. And . . . well, the terrible truth is I don't mind. I probably should, but I don't. There *is* a sense of satisfaction in clearing up and tidying away and making things sparkle. I haven't just been influenced by Mrs Hinch; the Shake'n'Vac lady got there first decades before, filling my head with dreams of dancing across the carpet with my vacuum, merrily spreading good smells.

Someone should do a PhD on what happens in the female brain when you bend down to tidy up a pair of men's pants, versus the impact of an encounter with discarded undergarments belonging to a child in your care. There is officially no excuse for either, that goes without saying. However, I would suggest the child's appalling, entitled behaviour may be quickly explained away; the man's not so much. But I do wonder. Am I indulging my own children now because I fear they may end up with their own unfair share of drudgery later in life? My student daughter tells me their male friends come over to their house to use the loo because they never have toilet paper. FOR GOD'S SAKE, BUY SOME.

In the interests of fairness, I should say I'd never descaled a kettle or a showerhead in my life until I got divorced. Oh, that man could descale. Whenever youngsters fantasise about adulthood with all its fruity promise (Fi could tell you all about that), no one ever thinks about stuff like this. And although I may indeed be one of the few people alive to have acknowledged my genuine interest in removing great gloopy plugs of human hair from the shower drain, I know I'm not televisual enough to get the gig. The Gregg (two g's) you need for that show, Fi, is Wallace. Stick him back in a hairnet and let him loose with a Lakeland Drain Weasel. I'll be watching.

Still can't believe she was in *Who's Who*.

11

TICK, TOK:

CLOCK-WATCHING, CHILDCARE AND THE WINDY PLAYGROUNDS OF DOOM

JANE

SATURDAY, 1.35 P.M. WE'RE CROUCHED, whispering, in the airing cupboard by the stepladder. We're playing hide and seek and waiting to be found. We've been here a while now; I wonder how long, exactly? Eight, nine minutes? You try telling a bolshy toddler that it's going to be a long wait. Unless you count the vermin, there's no one else in the house.

That time isn't just something I've idly plucked, by the way; it's lodged in my memory. Time, or more precisely the slow passage of it, is still what first comes to mind when I think about caring for very young children. It's a cop-out, of course, an inoffensive way of saying I some-times found those early days of childcare very dull. Yes, I'm afraid they were. And I am afraid that I'm a bit of a coward and I can't quite bring myself to say it directly. Let's see:

Caring for young children can be really boring.

It looks awful written down. I know to some the very notion, however carefully it's framed, is quite offensive.

But it was true, certainly in my experience, and I think we should all be allowed to say so if it applies. If anything, I think we owe it to our own children to tell the truth, without sugar-coating. Here goes – as a parent you will not necessarily trip in dazzling sunlight through fields of daisies; you will probably spend time trying to find spare capacity in an overflowing nappy bin at a soft-play centre. And you'll be bone-weary, and frequently a bit cross.

So enter the wise old woman, here to tell you to beware the small child whose obsessive interests bore you senseless; they grow up with incredible speed and soon find *you* very dull indeed, unless they need you to part with your security code urgently. This wizened old crone says something you'll have heard before: the days do indeed go very, very slowly; the years whizz by.

Oh, I've seen today's young parents in my local park – the ones too busy looking at their phones to notice their child's glee on the slide, or delight at a puddle. I've been shocked by the tiniest of babies, goggle-eyed and gripping iPads, while their carers sort through the sweatshirts in Zara. In MY day, things were different. Although, in fairness, I was there the very moment CBeebies opened. Yes, before 2001 you had to attempt parenting in Britain without it. Dark days; a time before Mr Tumble. We were reliant on videos. Disney's *Snow White and the Seven Dwarfs* was our magical place of safety, but I'm still haunted by the wafer-thin plot of 'Postman Pat Takes a Message', in which there's a bit of a mix-up with Reverend Timms's sister's arrival at a UK airport. This was all long before Pat tooled up inexplicably and got his own helicopter. I'm not even sure he was married to Sarah at the time. Come to think of it – did she marry him for his chopper?

If you're familiar with the genius of Harry Chapin, the American singer-songwriter, you'll know his dev-astating gut-punch of a song 'Cat's In the Cradle', in which he charts the course of a man's relationship with his son. Initially, Dad's far too busy working to pay the boy much attention. Never mind – the child eagerly takes whatever scraps he can get and worships his dad anyway, so it doesn't seem to matter. Until the day comes when the dad is old, and the tables are turned: the boy's grown up and too busy to see his old man. Long, long before I became a parent I used to shiver when I heard that song. There aren't many like it. Funny that. I suppose it's simply easier and more lucrative to write songs about lust and longing, rather than the price you pay for being a preoccupied, self-obsessive workaholic.

Filling up the days is the huge, blank chunk of parent-hood you don't give much thought to beforehand: a sub-ject they don't appear to cover at all at antenatal classes. Which, when you think about it, is ridiculous. Why didn't the perfectly nice, if frankly slightly irritating, woman in charge just say, 'Look everyone, this is a slog. Realistically, depending on the number of offspring you're blessed with, you're looking at a decade or more of sleep disrup-tion, shattered dreams and marital discord.' Instead, we got hours of playful chat about birth-plans, mucus plugs and nipple shields. Not a murmur about the everyday grind. The bit when you're woken up again at 5.37 a.m. and in spite of everything your first thought is, IS THIS IT???! The much-longed-for child is here, they're healthy, everyone says how lucky you are, and you know it's true and you know you are – but what are you actually going to *do* all day? What if it rains? And will you be any good at the business of caring for a small child?

Does anyone who's ever looked after a child really think of childcare as 'unskilled' work? Are you joking? Because my 'real' job consisted partly of reading out loud in an animated fashion, I thought I'd probably be OK at reading stories (I wasn't, particularly; they pre-ferred their grandmothers), but the rest of it felt alien and challenging. When I was eight or nine, and left in charge of the littler ones while the mums sat in swirly-carpeted lounges with steaming mugs of Nescafé sharing confi-dences and listening to Carly Simon or The Carpenters, I wanted desperately to be with the grown-ups, not stuck upstairs keeping a watching brief over yet another game of School. Although, God knows, that was preferable to Fairies. The latter didn't even involve scrap paper and felt-tips – there was no real supervisory role at all in Fairyland. Nothing suitable for someone of my obvious talent and calibre.

And much later, conversations around our future at my academic secondary school were always about careers. Our parents mostly had 'jobs', but we were a generation of pioneering young women, born in the 1960s, saddled with the label 'bright', and all called Jane, Fiona, Catherine, Susan or Sarah. Margaret Thatcher became Prime Minister when we were in our mid-teens; there were no limits, girls, not any more. Forget jobs, we would be having A Career. It was a huge responsibility, this, to be so very, very fortunate. We would have lives and chances our forebears couldn't have dreamed of. Good grief, my own great-great-grandmother had died giving birth to her fourteenth child, and here was I, with the chance of going to university. Woe betide any girl who did not take full advantage!

I know I benefited hugely from that brisk, aspirational approach to my future, but in retrospect it might have been a good idea for our education to consider a few more of the practicalities. I don't mean we should have had lessons on how to occupy the under-threes on unpromising Saturday afternoons in November, but perhaps we might have been encouraged to ponder the challenges of combining fulfilling working lives with raising children. It was simply never referred to. School wasn't really a place for those sorts of real-life discussions then. Nor did we have PSHCE, or what my children used to call 'Feelings'. I think the closest we got to that was the lesson on periods, but by the time that happened we'd all started them, and the teacher was quite elderly, and she had to ask us how many days they lasted for.

'Five days? As long as that? Good grief.'

You said it, love.

Anyway, I think I may already be in danger of reworking the age-old question 'Can you have it all?', to which the answer remains a resounding 'No'. But these days at least, we have the golden opportunity to work ourselves into a right old frenzy trying. If we're lucky, we may get a few years off to recharge before we're back on duty trying to help our daughters do the same.

By the way, my generation should acknowledge we dodged a parenting bullet – having older children during the pandemic may not have been entirely plain sailing, but I've lost count of the number of times I've thanked the Goddess of Fluke for my parenting good fortune. If this had all happened a decade ago, I'd have been home-schooling with the best – or worst – of them. I'd have dreaded the Ofsted visit, let's put it that way. And just yesterday, I saw a young woman in the window of her flat, in a dressing gown, holding a baby, watching what passes for the lockdown world going by. If she was jealous of me, even for a second, I wanted to tell her I'd just popped out for some baking parchment; I wasn't a bold adventurer out on the razzle.

We're still in the airing cupboard. It is lovely and warm in here. What time is it now? Twenty to?

Reasoning with the toddling community isn't easy. You try telling someone who's not quite two-and-a-half that games of hide and seek are best played when, well, there's someone else around to do the seeking. I would try to explain that we'd have a long time to wait here in the dark, it would get pretty boring, even if we did sing for a bit, and it might be better to do something else. The swings maybe?

After a tense period of negotiation, we'd leave the cupboard and venture downstairs. Good. It's now just after 1.45 p.m. Make a fuss of getting coats on, finding wellies, maybe sticking some apple slices in a bag . . . it could be two before we leave. Fantastic. Gradually eating up the day, bit by bit. We might meet someone we know. Or know a little. Or vaguely recognise. This period of your life isn't a time to be discerning, to be honest. You'd talk to anyone and, strangely, you find anyone would talk to you, too. Turns out they were in no position to be discerning either. This is the time in which you may acquire, by stealth, the Emergency Friend. A She'll Do (no, not you, Liz). You don't have to have a thing in common, apart from ownership of a buggy and a mutual interest in the impact of sleep deprivation. Hang on – Liz, was I your She'll Do?

You're not quite yourself any more; you're still learning to be someone else, someone who's just started a mammoth new job – the one she'll never finish; the one she knows she won't, or can't, get right. That much – if nothing else – seems certain.

I'm never surprised by women talking about the impact of postnatal depression; I'm just astonished some women say they didn't get it at all.

Was that really me, inadequately steering the pram around a circuit of Mothercare, a good five or six times, quietly dying inside, contemplating going up a teat size?

Maybe one more hole? It seemed quite a momentous decision, one I could never hope to make. Perspective has no part to play in this. You cannot tell yourself to relax, take the long view. You aren't to know that this tiny baby, stubbornly stuck on the ninth centile in the Red Book, really not that keen on SMA Gold, battling to get through her six ounces, will one day take up space in your kitchen, marinating tofu and listening to her 'music'. You are resolutely in the moment, helpless, lost, all at sea. It might have helped a bit if I'd been warned. Or maybe I was and didn't listen.

And don't forget, this was the early twenty-first century, long before social media sank its gnashers into motherhood and turned it into something else. A brand! Something you could even monetise as long as you did it stylishly, prettily enough. A few brave and clever souls may tell their brilliant truth on Instagram (thank you, Daisy May Cooper), but it's generally awash with the unachievable. A dire succession of perfect maternal moments, all a million miles away from elasticated waists, broken nights and brain fug.

Still, with luck it'll soon be teatime (5 p.m. sharp). Bath (6 p.m., 6.15 at the latest). Bed (7 p.m.). The woman who was almost teetotal before all this leans back against a kitchen unit and sinks her first well-deserved drink: 7.05 p.m. Phew – day done. Off-duty until . . . let's not think about tomorrow morning now.

I know this sounds stupid, but I honestly hadn't realised how much there was to this parenting business. The practical stuff that had to be done; the emotional impact of a new, helpless creature entirely reliant on you. That's you, the person no one had ever relied on for anything of any real significance. I had no idea how much time I'd spend caring, and I didn't know how much I'd . . . care. That's absurd, but there we are. I still live close to my daughters' primary school, and on a good day with the right wind direction I can hear the unmistakable clamour of the playground. But every time I pass the place, I have two very distinct memories.

On my youngest daughter's first day of school, I made the mistake on purpose of walking past at lunchtime. And unfortunately I got what I wanted, a glimpse of her. She was entirely alone, unmistakable blonde mop, her finger in her mouth as groups of other children swirled around her. I hurried on, an emotional wreck. Later, she said it had been fun, she liked it.

I'm not sure that was worse than when her big sister conducted her first Show and Tell in Reception, taking in her carefully curated stick collection. The event had been much anticipated, and on the way home that afternoon I asked how it had gone.

Silence. Then, 'No one had any questions.'

Bloody hell, that still makes me cross. She had some really good sticks.

But before you know it, you're no longer anywhere near the centre of their world. They inhabit another place altogether. Their sticks have all been thrown away, and they didn't even notice. They make references to things you know nothing about, worship musical artistes you rather like but secretly think sound quite a lot like someone who was big in the 1980s, and then one day, you need to ask them for help. They are Computer Support.

They start moving around independently. Well, until they need you to bring them home . . .

'Heycanyoupickmeup?' (Usually all one word, like that.)

'Where are you?'

'We're at that place.'

'We?'

'Ugh, you know, like, everyone?'

'Which place?'

'That place we went to once. Well no, it's basically actually by that place. Can you come now?'

'I'll try but I still don't really know . . .'

'I told you yesterday and my phone's out of charge so can you just come?'

I went, obviously. I even found her. And picking them up in a car is always good because communication without eye contact seems easier for all concerned. And this is just the beginning of the where-the-hell-are-they-now-and-when-will-they-be-back years. If you have daughters, you might also get you-can't-go-out-dressed-like-that. This is where feminism and reality meet and find each other wanting. They want to dress in a certain way, but they can't go out like that. You wish they could; you know they can't. Nerves of steel and huge reserves of patience are required. Sometimes, you find yourself thinking fondly of winding the bobbin up. OK, maybe it never gets quite that bad.

Life with teenagers does often seem like a succession of missed opportunities to engage, best illustrated by a smartphone being thrust under your nose when you're peeling spuds with the instruction to 'Look at this now!'. You're hugely flattered by the attention – after all, you haven't seen them for, what is it, three hours? – but you can't find your glasses (yes, they may indeed be on your head) and when you're finally able to focus, you're faced with a short video clip of a young person being witty, or making a very serious political point indeed, through the thoroughly modern medium of TikTok. Your challenge is to judge, very quickly, which one of those it is. The pressure is immense. React in the wrong way, and another moment of engagement is lost. They're back upstairs again. You're a waste of space, not worth wasting time on. You feel hopeless.

If you're lucky, you can always ring your mother. If she's not busy she'll always talk to you.

FI

I'M INTRIGUED AT YOUR INGENUITY in suggesting a game of hide and seek when there's no one coming to seek. It shows a certain amount of genius. Did it extend to other kids' games? I'm imagining that playing Sleeping Lions at yours might have involved leaving them to pretend to sleep for . . . er . . . an hour? Pass-the-parcel where there's just a note in the final layer saying you have to go to Bethnal Green Sorting Office next Monday between 8 a.m. and 2 p.m. to pick it up? Brilliant, sister. Brilliant.

Oh God. Early years childcare. Not my forte either, I'm afraid, and in fact I'm somewhat reluctant to even go back there in my head. I am always rather heartened to hear of anyone else who struggled their way through it. It's a bonding badge of the highest order – the one marked Honesty. I also know that I found a bit of myself, and a couple of my closest friends too, in that shared experience of the desultory playground on a wet Wednesday morning at the witching hour. It sounds as if your witchy ones were later in the day – my unfathomable sixty minutes always seemed to lie between 10 and 11 a.m. You'd been up since silly o'clock and it wasn't even time for lunch. The squeaky swings. The merry-go-round of vomit. Yikes. Eyes darting around the playground in the hope of catching another darting eye in which you could see your whole existence reflected. A look from mother to mother that says, 'Are you so stressed that you could eat your own hands? Oh, hello friend.'

Looking back on those early years, I can see now that some of my problems were of my own making. Nearly two decades of work had ingrained in me a certain formula of Method, Results, Conclusion. I think most of my life was based on the premise of my Year 7 chemistry lessons. In adult life that translated into putting the right ingredients together – hard work and concentration – performing your tasks – like you, that means reading out loud and chatting to people – and the conclusion should be that you not only get paid, you get to leave at the end of the day.

Nothing prepared me for how far away from that life new motherhood is. There is no method to it, despite what gurus like Gina Ford might tell you. I had as much chance of getting my babies to sleep and eat at my bidding as I did of climbing Kathmandu in a pair of flip-flops. And most days felt like that. Parenting isn't a destination, it is a lifelong journey. And if you ever find yourself sitting in soft play with someone intoning that at you, then just move away very quickly. Because there is a lot of intoning advice – and a whole massive industry around early-years parenting – but it is also really up to you to find your own way of doing it. All I would say is keep the bar very low on what you can achieve every day. And find like-minded souls to share a lot of that day with. There are all kinds of parents out there, and spending time with those who do it very differently to you, or make you feel bad about how you are doing it, will only make it harder.

And your own life, with all its essential ingredients, will carry on in the background of those years, something that no book or show or guru will have factored in. My adored dad died, suddenly, just five weeks before my son was born, and I found myself balancing a pot of sorrow in one hand and a jar of joy in the other – as well as holding on very tight to a newborn baby. As anyone with even Key Stage 1 Empathy will be able to see, it wasn't ideal. Don't worry, though, I never dropped the baby. Both those things – birth and death – stretch you in ways you will never understand until they happen. I'm not sure I quite know what did happen in those first few months. It would be nice to say that I came through it all older and wiser, but I'm not sure that was the case really. More tired maybe. More alive. Sadder and happier at the same time. Is that even possible? The endless modern search to find a positive in the negative is not my cup of tea, so I won't bother if that's all right with you. All I really know is that the centrifuge of my life moved as it does for every parent who has a child, and every child who stops having a parent. And although I very much wanted that centrifugal force to be firmly planted in making a home and a new little family, actually being alone at home felt unbearable, so as soon as I and my tiny son could go out, out we went.

We went anywhere that would have us. Playgrounds, church hall groups, something called Monkey Music, storytelling sessions in libraries – anything with baby in the title. The other thing you don't know about until it happens, and by then it is too late to go back, is the return of tambourines. You can go for decades in adult life without hearing a tambourine – but have a baby and they are everywhere. It's very cruel. Let's just say it's not the instrument of choice for the caffeine-wired, sleep-deprived, hormonal woman.

The tambourine featured quite strongly in a class called something like Tick Tock in my neck of the woods. It involved singing and clapping and lots of parents and babies in a very big church hall and it had been recommended to me in hushed tones. 'Oh *everyone* goes to it.' Excellent, I thought. A chance to meet other grown-ups. Something to do on a wet Wednesday. A chance to let my lovely little crawler crawl around. I booked in. Now, leaving the house with a baby is fraught. It takes an age and no one really knows why. There are bottles and bags and nappies and bananas to pack up, and even though you have those things to hand every day it still seems like you are setting off on an expedition to rival Shackleton's in order to just make it out of the front door. I managed it though. But then the bus was a bit late. And I'd been up since five. And I got to the church hall and pushed open the door to see a whole circle of mums (sorry, but there just weren't any dads) and the whole class stopped. And the woman running it said, 'You're late' – to which I think I just carried on bumping my way with buggy and baby through the door. I mean, it's not a sitting of the High Court or a radio show or something of extreme mega-importance like that. So what if I was a bit tardy? But she said, 'You're late, we've started. You'll have to come back next week.' Everyone just stared at me. And I actually burst into tears. All that effort. All that packing. All that frigging hope.

And the even worse thing – the thing that tells you everything about the different time warp that new motherhood puts you in – was that I was so bewildered by it all that *I did go back the next week.* And guess what? It was rubbish. The woman stood at the front and did all her songs, backed up by a sad-looking young man on the guitar. The mums had to hang on to their crawling babies – WHO WEREN'T ALLOWED TO MOVE AROUND but just had to be jigged up and down to the 'music'. It cost a fortune and you had to sign up for a whole 'term'. Like it was Eton. I didn't. But when your audience is comatose with wet-wipe fumes and hasn't finished either a sentence or their own sandwich or had more than three hours' consecutive kip in a year, I guess you can ask for whatever you like.

So much of early-years childcare is like that. Disorientating. Odd. A bit mind-bending. With unbelievable shafts of joy. It took having another baby to learn to just stay home and eat biscuits. And to just accept a major shift in identity.

I couldn't really work out who I was when my kids were tiny. I knew that it was the start of something different for all of us, but where I was in that morass took a long time to get a handle on. In fact, it took leaving paid work to do the harder full-time home work to realise that I wasn't very good at doing it full-time. And that it was really fine to do that. Ever since I have straddled two worlds rather badly, as most of us do – being the woman in the office who works around her kids and being the parent in the playground who parents around her work. That's two whole audiences of people who can judge me and find me wanting. Yay! I'll never really figure out what is 'best'. Who does? Does anyone know any parent who is 'having it all'? The notion that simply by having a job as well as kids you are attempting a feat of greed is so daft. No one says of a man that by having a job and kids he is demanding something unattainable in the world.

But that's the thing I learned in the windy playgrounds at doom o'clock – to just go with the flow in life a bit more. Does it matter what people think? It's hard enough to find the right current, let alone perfect a stroke while in it. For me, being half one thing and half the other is where I've ended up. Some days are good in each different world. Some days not so much.

And what will I tell my kids about the early years experience? Like you – the truth. At least how it was for me. And, as with everything now, I hope the gender matrix is changing, and if it turns out that my son is better suited to being at home and wiping things then he can be the one to step away from his work/career with no judgement, none of the angst, none of the uncertainty that faces new mums. And also really enjoy it, if that's what makes him tick.

I will try not to be too negative, though. There is a current mum fashion to provide a running commentary on how shite everything can be which, although heartening in its honesty, is also a bit depressing. Kids changed my life, undoubtedly for the better. I can moan about aspects of it all because then the moment passes. And the bits of joy have far outweighed the moments of pain, something that I don't want *not* to be able to say just in case it sounds smug, or out of the current vogue. The only thing that I really, really do know is that for those women who have wanted this life and have not been able to have it, all of this must seem such a self-indulgent whinge. I have no idea how I would have fared if I hadn't had kids. Badly, I suspect. I try to think of that as often as I can when I am knee-deep in attempting to fold lycra sports kit, offering advice about periods (and what advice *is* there for something so boringly painful and incapacitating, do let me know because I am still struggling with that), getting through my own infernal parental controls and disguising vegetables in pies.

I suspect I may well have gone into a cupboard and never come out.

By the way, are you still in there? Shall I come and get you out?

12

THINGS I WISH I'D KNOWN BEFORE LEAVING HOME:

'NO ONE NEEDS A LIMONCELLO'

FI

THERE'S A LOT OF NOISE BEFORE you leave home. It's often in the form of endless questions. Have you sorted out some accommodation? When are you actually off? Do you have a positive attitude to the world that will be enough to see you through? Will you call when you get there? (This usually refers to a place, not 'Will you call when you get to the adult world?', although I think that might be the call your parents actually want.)

Everyone tells you you're a grown-up, but in the same tone of voice they've used since you were twelve.

You think you know everything. You'd be fed up with people telling you that you don't know everything if only you weren't so convinced that you do.

But perhaps it might be one thing that we can all agree on much further down the line – that when we were young we didn't know much at all. If you have got to midlife and believe that you did know it all when you were eighteen or twenty, then I'd rather not sit next to you at dinner/supper/tea if you don't mind. You must be an almighty wazzock.

There's way more distraction around these days, too. It must be confusing to the young adult that 'life skills' now seems to be more about learning to visualise the heat inside you at a Candlelit Hot Stone Meditation Sound Bath session in a local 'wellbeing centre' than learning how to change a fuse in a plug without electrocuting yourself or setting fire to the house. There's no point in being able to visualise the fire inside you if in fact you are on fire at the time.

I'm pretty sure that I ignored anything my parents said to me between the ages of fifteen and twenty-five, but if those same words had been told to me by literally anyone else then I might actually have listened.

So here is a list of genuine things I wish I had known before leaving home at the tender age of seventeen, released like a dove in a Bonnie Tyler video into the wind machine of life. I might as well leave it here, because I suspect my children will be ignoring it:

1. Don't leave home at seventeen. If you can help it. Spend as much time in the proving drawer as you can. The final bake will be better. It's not always possible, I know. It wasn't for me. But don't rush out if you don't have to.
2. If the chicken smells off, it probably is.
3. If he smells off, he probably is.
4. If you smell off, go and see a doctor.

5. Most of the time it is sensible to do what the
   doctor says. For example, always finish the
   course of antibiotics. I had simple, albeit painful,
   tonsillitis in my twenties. I didn't finish a course of
   antibiotics and I went back to work within three
   days. I ended up with a 'quinsy' tonsil – and, yup,
   that sounds Dickensian because it is. It resulted
   in a doctor having to pop it open with a scalpel.
   Imagine *The Exorcist* and you are there. I was in a
   hospital in Dundee for longer than I cared to be.
   I have nothing against Dundee, it's a delightful
   city. It's the birthplace of Lorraine Kelly AND the
   resting place of the *Discovery* – but I don't live in
   Dundee, nor did any of my friends, and if I'd just
   stayed home for another four days and finished the
   course . . . etc. etc. Repeat to fade.

6. While we're on the health thing – for heaven's sake
   learn some first aid. Don't be one of those people
   who 'didn't know what to do'. You don't have to
   train to be on a St John's Ambulance team, but
   why on earth wouldn't you learn how to save a life
   if needed?

7. Read Anne Tyler. I can't quote great chunks of
   her wisdom – or even name her characters – but I
   know that all she has written about relationships
   and family life has stayed with me and informs
   many of my decisions without me realising it.
   I think it's called redundant wisdom, isn't it?
   It's the stuff that we put in our heads and don't

always use but can call on when we need to. It's like central heating for the mind. I'd also highly recommend anything by Elizabeth Strout, Maggie O'Farrell, Nora Ephron, Nick Hornby and a bit of Siri Hustvedt, too. (Although I think Hustvedt is the ginger shot at the juice bar, so don't worry if you can't take a whole one.)

8. Lovers will make you high, friends will make you happy.

9. Never sacrifice the latter for the former.

10. While we're on the love boat – if he/she says he/she loves you within a week of meeting you, it's probably love that he/she loves more than he/she actually loves you. Beware of the lover who loves love. And good luck with that sentence.

11. I'd say give drugs a swerve, at least until they are legal. It won't be long. In the meantime, if you wouldn't buy your mince from a bloke on the corner of London Fields, why would you buy anything else from him? And know that you are part of a chain that costs other people further down the line way more than it probably costs you. Know that they do different things to different people. And they might not be for you.

12. No one really cares about cellulite apart from you, and you can't even see it most of the time, so is it worth worrying about?

13. Avoid changing rooms with mirrors where you can

see your cellulite just on the off chance that No. 12 has started to bother you.

14. Have you ever, and I mean ever, not liked a friend of yours because they have put on or lost a few pounds? Did you love your parents/aunts/favourite teachers any the less when they got wrinkles? Nope. So please don't think about laying that judgement on yourself.

15. Don't reheat rice. Or if you do, reheat it in a microwave until it is like tiny pellets of hardened uncooked rice that appear to be inedible. Then they will be inedible. This method makes sure that you throw it away.

16. If a pair of shoes is too tight in the shop, they will always be too tight. Walk away, sister, just walk away.

17. Ask lots of questions. Then actually listen to the answers.

18. Saying sorry feels good as long as you mean it. Saying sorry when you don't mean it will turn you into a pain.

19. Get pets and look after them well. It's worth it.

20. Don't get houseplants. No matter how well you look after them they will die and it won't have been worth it.

21. Parking fines don't pay themselves.

22. Avoid peach schnapps.

23. The expression 'first impressions count' is bollocks. I have close friends whom I couldn't

stand when I first met them. I now love them. Some people get nervous when they meet people for the first time. Some people are just having a rubbish day. Friendship is like feeding broccoli to a three-year-old – you do have to give it at least a couple of tries.

24. Kindness is next to wisdom. Find kind people and stay close. Possibly consider being the kind person yourself.

25. The saying 'A change is as good as a rest' is bollocks, too. Often in life I have found sleep is exactly the answer.

This chapter is short because I am going to have a small kip.

JANE

LET'S DEAL WITH SOME OF THE SPECIFICS FIRST.

You're right about a great deal here – jolly well done. You've certainly nailed the big stuff on love, pets and books. But wrong on houseplants, I'm afraid. I've started to invest in these lately and they're surprisingly forgiving. And, I think, they can lend a faintly bohemian air to what we now call a 'space'. And when they dry up or the cat attacks them in a fit of feline pique, just buy another, you tight-fisted twit.

Peach schnapps? Right again. I would also add to

the list any alcoholic drink of a novelty colour, Pernod, obviously, and Limoncello (even if you have all had a 'great night' and you feel an urgent need to 'round it off', NO ONE NEEDS A LIMONCELLO). Also: any form of Croatian fig brandy. That'll rattle right through your Balkans, I can assure you.

Just Say NO was the anti-drugs campaign of our youth, but I think Fi's mince analogy works just as well. In fact it works brilliantly well for me, a lifelong opponent of gristle. Just the thought of buying a pound of beef mince off someone who lurks on street corners at night – no ta. I speak as someone whose go-to dish was very much mince, and who owns a copy of that seminal work, *Mighty Mince Cookbook* by Jane Todd. I may run a vegetarian household these days (occasional fish-eating permitted), but I have very fond memories of the wholesome flirting involved in ordering from my local butcher. I don't know what it is about the rather charged atmosphere of a shop full of animal carcasses and muscular men with bloody white coats, watching on appreciatively while Young Terry chooses you a nice plump pork chop. Just me? All I'll say is you don't get that in the greengrocer's. Maybe just because aubergines really are much of a muchness.

By the way, I wasn't ever into drugs, no.

As for calling when you get to adulthood, you've got me there. I think I'm probably still at the services, nursing an overpriced coffee and thinking about splashing out on a new in-car air freshener. I know I'm older (despite all your sound advice about cellulite, I'm only too well aware of the mounting evidence), but the wisdom and the certainty I was expecting to find as an adult haven't turned up yet. I'm still not the person I'd turn to for advice.

I used to leave home regularly as a very small child, hurling a few skinny-ribs in a tartan holdall with my teddy. I was woefully misunderstood, and it was high time I made my own way in the world. The rest of the household got on with their dinner and after a few minutes freezing on the doorstep I stood on tiptoe, rang the bell, and was usually readmitted without a word being said. It was a long walk back up the stairs, trying to retain my dignity as I put teddy back in his place on my bed and squashed the jumpers back in the drawer. Maybe next time.

When I did it for real, I was eighteen and heading for university. Mum had packed me two mugs. One was for me, the other 'in case you make a friend'. I think low expectations are a good thing on the whole. She also warned me not to go to bed with wet hair. My sister didn't come to the door to see me off; she was busy dragging all her belongings across the landing, laying claim to the biggest bedroom at last. No doubt she was mourning my departure in her own way. Dad drove, full of blood-curdling tales of his National Service in Nottinghamshire in the 1950s, apparently to reassure me. He'd seen off the Russians all right. I didn't know much about what to expect but sensed that freshers' week in

Birmingham probably wouldn't involve fending off Commies. There was a toga party though, and a Cheese and Wine Mingle.

You're right, Fi. Seventeen is too young. I think eighteen is young. Though maybe I was just a very young eighteen. I think twenty-five might be about right, if everyone involved can stand it that long. But that assumes everyone has a home prepared to accommodate them, and I know now that isn't true. Another thing I also know is that my fixed, predictable, solid family home was a mighty blessing I simply took for granted. I mocked it and was glad to be free of it, but I always knew it was there. Still there. I could always go back, and they'd let me in.

13

BRAVE FACE:

NERVES, VULNERABILITY AND BOOTS QUIZZES

JANE

JANUARY 2021.

Deep in the pandemic, a jaunty promotional email arrives from Boots. That's Boots the well-known high street chemist, purveyors of corn plasters and luxurious facial serums.

'Let's talk mental health!'

Yes, let's. These days I sometimes think we talk of little else. The email's tone is chatty and positive. Nothing to fear here. The images show people in very early middle age, all of whom live in bright, airy accommodation. There's a bearded man sitting cross-legged, eyes firmly shut, in deep contemplation. His dog is fast asleep on quite a pricey-looking grey sofa behind him. I wonder whether I'd let a large dog occupy a sofa like that. I think the answer is no. We are told he is 'rebooting'. The man, not his dog. Don't be silly.

Next, a woman in chunky headphones gazes out of a window, her attractive pot plant also in view. Houseplants are having a moment, and so is she. Be gone, aspidistras, they speak of shattered dreams and spinsterhood; hello the happy houseplant, green and full of promise. The email says this lucky lady is enjoying some 'headspace'. I wonder what she's listening to. I hope for her sake it's not the news. Probably not 'Dance Yourself Dizzy' by Liquid Gold or *The Best of The Dooleys* either, judging by her thoughtful expression. A bit of light classical, I think. Debussy?

The email invites me to consider meditation. 'It's about managing everyday stress, keeping calm and giving you the tools . . . to deal with your anxieties and worries.' Tools. I've got a couple of screwdrivers and at least three bunches of Allen keys, all bought when I couldn't find any Allen keys. But they're not the same thing. This is serious. The email has moved on to mindfulness. Which I'm told will help 'navigate difficult emotions'. By now, in spite of myself, I am interested. God knows, I'm both anxious and worried, I'd like to live in a minimalist flat with views, and I find navigating difficult emotions very hard indeed. Give me the tools, Boots! But then they go and ruin it by promising to 'topline some key features'.

Oh no you won't, not on my watch. I have to stop reading for a while. Too much twenty-first-century babble for this twentieth-century brain. But the promise is irresistible tosh, and I'm back after a brew and a few gobbled slices of extra-mature cheddar, a bit of mindless (not mindful) eating.

There's a Wellbeing quiz further down the email. It's in full association with Public Health England, which is reassuring, and starts by asking how I'm feeling, on a sliding scale from 'really knackered' to 'full of beans'. I'm rather startled by the colloquial use of 'knackered' here, for some reason. It's not quite what I expect from Boots or Public Health England. Still, I answer truthfully and place myself very firmly in the middle. No one who knows me well would ever describe me as being full of beans. Mildly enthusiastic, occasionally, if a full roast dinner I haven't cooked comes into view; or Anne Tyler has a new book out. Nor could I realistically claim to be knackered when I make my living by talking or, more accurately, sitting at a laptop in athleisure, panicking.

I plough on. One of the questions is 'Apart from not getting ill, what are your health priorities?' One of the options offered is 'Fitting into my jeans.' I take a dim view of this initially, and then realise it is something I do indeed care about. Unfortunately.

The quiz is a long, fuzzy haul, but I don't cheat. Well, apart from exaggerating my fruit and veg intake slightly, by taking a generous view of my passion for individual sherry trifles. Which sometimes contain fruit. Or traces of fruit, if they're made in the same factory as the individual fruit trifles, and let's face it, they probably are.

The quiz is over. Boots and Public Health England deliver their verdict.

'Sounds like you're not feeling positive or negative as far as your wellbeing's concerned, Jane, so maybe you could do with a bit of a shake-up?'

It's the story of my life. Straight down the line, bang in the middle. Not even the combined intellectual heft of Britain's leading high-street chemist and no less a body than Public Health England can place me anywhere interesting. And that chummy tone grates – don't call me Jane, stupid email quiz. I know it's my name and I had to tell you what my name was to do the damn quiz, but don't call me Jane. And what constitutes a 'shake-up' in this context, exactly? I hate that term. It's in my bin of clever nonsense, along with 'stakeholder' and 'going forwards'. I suppose I could change my go-to cheese from life-limiting hard to healthy, sensible, revolting cottage. But perhaps I'll wait for happier times. Or, as a British politician in 2021 would say, 'the happier times that surely lie ahead'. Oh, surely. Until then, I'll have to find other ways to shake myself up. Perhaps I'll start by buying some high-quality cushioned headphones (from Boots?) and staring out of the window.

But more importantly, leading high-street chemist, you started by offering to talk about the serious issue of mental health, and we have somehow wound up at the place we call Wellbeing. It's a very modern muddle. Wellbeing is nicer, certainly; it suggests a cosy world of self-care: cuddly throws in neutral shades, a silky bath foam, perhaps one of those huge, scented candles. Stuff, in fact. Some of the stuff you could buy in, say, a leading high-street chemist like Boots. Probably just a coincidence. And as it happens, I love all three of these self-care purchases. And yes, all three probably contribute to my wellbeing – just not as much as very strong, pre-sliced cheddar cheese.

But that's a rather facile point. And, frankly, typical of me. I am resistant to most talk of emotion and find the current preoccupation with oversharing quite unnerving. There are other things, of much more significance, that help to explain why I am indeed reasonably 'well'. Let's start with the obvious – good physical health, no money problems, a safe place to live, a stable childhood. The older I get, the more people I meet, the more uncomplicated my start in life appears to have been. Don't forget that if it's the same for you. I know I sometimes do. And then there's pure luck. There's no accounting for why some of us have so much more of that than others. When a friend of mine spent time in a psychiatric hospital a few years ago, she told me that almost no one else she met there had ever had a job. They were mentally ill, certainly, and needed care, but they were also long-term sufferers of that chronic condition Shit Life Syndrome.

I've only been inside a psychiatric hospital once. In the late 1980s the vast old asylums were finally closing and 'care in the community' was a bold new approach. I was going to meet the handful of patients still living at the huge local hospital, once home to over 1,000 people. They were about to be moved to a much more convivial, and much smaller, 'care setting'.

Powick Hospital had opened in 1852 as the Worcester City and County Pauper Lunatic Asylum. It was just off the main road between Worcester and the spa town of Malvern; you could see the hills from the grounds. Its history is fascinating – Edward Elgar had famously worked there, conducting the asylum band; it had been the home of all sorts of pioneering and controversial research, some of it involving LSD; but a cursory Google also revealed that it had featured on the brilliant Granada TV documentary programme *World in Action* in 1968. Had I known that – and sat through the harrowing footage then – I'm not sure I'd have approached my reporting assignment quite so cheerily.

You can watch the documentary yourself on YouTube, but I must warn you it's the stuff of nightmares. The black and white film is all shot on a long-term female ward, F13, home to an uncertain number of bedraggled, toothless old souls, some crying pitifully, others lost – or trapped – in thought. The staff are the wrong side of brusque, the ward stinks of urine. One woman tells the reporter she's been there forty-four years, and it was, simply, 'hell'. Why were the cameras let in? The ward sister, crisp uniform, rather a defensive manner, admits it's truly dreadful, but what can they do? She's asked what relatives make of it, and it's then she mentions shame. Oh, the shame of it all. The shame of being connected to anyone who winds up here. In this state.

I certainly didn't see anything like this in 1989, just some rather frail, rheumy-eyed ladies who'd been there far, far too long to be able to make a life for themselves on their own. Why they'd been sent there in the first place was, in some cases, a total mystery. I recall being told that some of them may have been merely considered 'headstrong'. Or they'd been inconveniently pregnant. I wonder whether their families felt any shame. I'd naively imagined I might be able to get some of them on tape, reminiscing, chatting about the old days.

'Hello there! How do you feel?'

Can you imagine? Even I wasn't that stupid. The staff seemed caring and attentive. But who was I to judge? I'd just barrelled up in my BBC local-radio-station-branded white Vauxhall Astra, trusty Uher tape recorder slung over my shoulder. Sometimes, honestly, journalism is wasted on the young.

There are luxury flats and a housing estate on the site of the hospital now. Young girls are no longer incarcerated for decades, and we all inhabit a world where the very grandest people speak about removing the stigma around mental health.

Not everyone's on message. There are the Old-Schoolers: 'Counselling!!! Everyone's offered bloody counselling these days, aren't they? It's a load of nonsense! You only have to be near the scene of a minor collision between a milk float and a lad on a moped and before you know it, you're flat on your back on a chaise longue in a room with a sea-breeze diffuser and a nice woman called Phoebe, being encouraged to "talk about how you feel".'

The clear implication here is that this has all gone too far, and we must pull ourselves together and look on the bright side like we used to. Count your blessings! Back then, people dealt with little bits of unpleasantness by keeping quiet, or resorting to strong drink, or a bit of violence. The good old days. But if you really still think like that, you're swimming against the tide.

'Mental health' was referenced freely and frequently throughout the pandemic, and I certainly don't think that's a bad thing. I don't think anyone spoke of mental health a century ago during the Spanish Flu. Perhaps it wouldn't even have been the case if all this had happened in the 1980s, or even the 1990s. Would there really have been endless references then to 'the impact of all this on our mental health'? I very much doubt it.

So we are making progress. Some of the shame has gone. Mental health is so much a part of the national conversation, you might assume there's been a dramatic improvement in services. Not yet, apparently – ask anyone trying to access them.

I should say I do still reserve the right to feel profoundly cynical about the modern classic, the Celebrity Opening Up. This usually takes the form of a well-timed and sympathetic interview coinciding with a new book, film or TV show. There have been so many of these in recent years you could be forgiven for thinking success in some areas of our national life is simply not possible without waging a private battle of one sort or another. A private battle a celebrity has suddenly decided to make very public, no doubt reluctantly.

As I type, schools are shut to all but vulnerable children and the children of key workers. My own seventeen-year-old may never actually go to school again, I realised in the middle of another restless night a few days ago. I'm not sure she knows that; I won't mention it. It's too sad. Perhaps I should mention it? But she seems robust enough; quite happy even. She jokes about her good fortune in having divorced parents, allowing her to visit her dad in another location during lockdown. I still hear the unmistakable, joyous racket of teenage girls' laughter from her bedroom as she talks to friends. She's at a Zoom eighteenth birthday party right now. The girl's mother left an individual party bag on the doorstep earlier – tiny bottle of Prosecco, a tube of Love Hearts, a small bag of Party Rings (accidentally vegan, in case you didn't know). The Prosecco has already taken effect – I've just asked her to keep it down a bit. Maybe she's one of the lucky ones, too. I hope they all are. Still, an eighteenth birthday party, on Zoom.

We are told, I'm sure quite rightly, that all this is causing a 'mental-health time bomb' for young people. All this *is* so much harder on the young and, I think, the very elderly too. But the young will still be feeling the effects decades from now. And perhaps they're more photogenic.

I heard some schoolgirls on a radio news programme yesterday, discussing – what else? – their feelings. They were missing their friends, missing face-to-face contact with teachers, but seemed resigned and rather sad; not angry, and not complaining. One articulate girl called Kitty tried to be positive – she didn't think there had been 'much of an impact on my mental health'. Kitty was eleven. I had to listen back to check. No, she really was eleven, and already quite fluent in a language I still trip up in.

Kitty was in school Year 6, so in ordinary times would be bracing herself for the ordeal of leaving primary school and going on to a secondary. This can now take the form of an extraordinarily emotional leaving assembly, with singing dinner ladies dancing around with ladles, filmed tributes, signed school polo shirts and parents in emotional freefall, clutching each other and wailing 'Where DID the time go?'

I was eleven in 1975 and have no memory of any sort of fuss when we left primary. We just didn't go any more. Have I got that right? I'm sure there was an assembly, a hymn and some words of encouragement . . . but crying and hugging and dancing dinner ladies? No. Somehow, in my lifetime, high emotion has entered British life, taken root, and now there's no escape.

When I was eleven, I didn't know I had any mental health, good or bad. No one ever mentioned the concept at all, which makes the omnipresent nature of it now so surprising to some people of my generation. I knew people had Nerves, and I knew enough to know that Nerves were best avoided. Conversations about people – they were usually women – with the condition Nerves were generally in whispers, and code. They sounded fascinating, frankly. 'Oooooh, she's off with her Nerves.' 'She's had a tough time after Frank, terrible lumbago and that trouble with her Nerves.'

Confusingly, this was very different to people who 'had a nerve'. As far as I could make out, the plural was undesirable and the singular was a damn cheek. No one in the immediate family had Nerves, but I did think I might get them, because I quite often suffered from something called a Nervous Tummy. That sounded a bit ominous to me. How long would it be before I too was 'off with my Nerves'? And where would I go?

This was not something I wanted. There didn't appear to be any treatment and your prospects were poor, plus there was the additional burden of other people lowering their voices and having very enjoyable conversations about you.

A good alternative to Nerves was a Brave Face, which was a more dignified way of meeting life's challenges. You could deal with every shot across the bows, from an unfortunate tumble in the playground to a family bereavement, by simply slapping a stoical expression on your chops and moving onwards. And if someone else had a spot of bother, then the best and kindest approach was surely to ignore the whole unfortunate business. Why remind someone their poor mother had died by offering your sympathy? It wouldn't do to express much interest. A bit nosy. They wouldn't want to be reminded, surely.

I've never forgotten a man I once interviewed on Radio 5 Live. It was the anniversary of the liberation of Belsen, and he'd been one of the first British soldiers to enter the concentration camp in 1945. I asked him to describe what he'd seen that day, and he did, speaking without pause or interruption for almost fifteen minutes. What he said was devastating, of course, but you could also hear the relief in his voice; he was glad to get the chance to go through it all again. After the war he'd gone home, and I wondered what his family had made of his experience. It was a lot to take in.

'Oh,' he said. 'Nobody ever asked. I think it was too much to take.'

My paternal grandfather was a short, quite gruff, occasionally rather pompous old chap in a hand-knitted zip-up cardigan who smoked a pipe and listened to John Arlott's cricket commentaries. One of his favourite songs was Rolf Harris's 'Two Little Boys'. If you leave Harris aside – and we must – it's a very touching song about childhood friends who play soldiers as children and fight alongside each other in battle as young men. Grandad joined the South Lancashire Regiment in his teens – I think he was sixteen – and was taken prisoner in the First World War. Beyond that, I can't tell you anything about his wartime experiences. I'm not saying he was any sort of hero. We don't know any more because he 'didn't talk about it'. In my imagined version of this story, I have of course cast myself as the person who might at least have asked him about it. He died when I was nine, so it's easy for me to play that game.

Somehow, those of us who grew up wearing a Brave Face, perhaps more often than we really wanted to, have ended up here, in this foreign country where everyone is speaking their truth and spilling their beans. We've gone from never talking about anything to talking about everything. Are there any secrets left? And are we really any happier?

Anyway, like I say, I'm fine. Thanks for asking.

FI

I THINK IT DOES ALL lie in the asking, not the telling. Although now I am going to tell you a little story, so make of that conundrum what you will.

In order to do so, I'd like to make a small withdrawal from the bank of radio shows past.

When I am not fannying around having the time of my life on the *Fortunately* podcast with you, I make a programme for the BBC World Service called *My Perfect Country*. The conceit is a simple one, but I like my radio shows to be simple. And I am conceited. Ha ha. In the series we are building a 'perfect country' using only the bits of other countries that actually work. It's a way of spinning the globe and stopping off in the company of people who have solved things. It's what is now called 'constructive journalism', which always makes me raise my eyebrows to Swiss clinic level because the implication is that, if left to settle, most journalism is not constructive and I disagree with that quite strongly. But, stay on point woman: *My Perfect Country* is probably a little bit like your mental-health pamphlet email minus the bearded man and the happy houseplants in its intent because it is delivering an intellectual wellness episode every time you listen to it.

One of the programmes that will remain with me forever was about modern attitudes to mental health and a hospital group in Michigan, which pioneered a 'zero-suicide program'. Although our health systems are different – and this is not one 'free at the point of care' like our NHS is – it's been recognised as one of the best ways to tackle poor mental health, and loads of countries have used the blueprint. It now has capital letters and 'Zero Suicide Policy' has been adopted in the UK; you might be interested to know that the first board to put it into practice was the Mersey NHS Trust in 2015. I know. Literally everything good is in the Greater Liverpool postcode. Back to Detroit in 2001, though, where the health-care system was struggling with the enormous increase in poor mental health, and depression in particular. And you could see why. The city had sunk from being one of the finest on earth – home to a car industry that gleamed with hope and optimism and literally sold the American Dream. It was home to Motown, too. You could work all day and sing along all night. In its heyday Detroit was shiny. It was where you went to make your life better.

But then, like a modern morality tale unfolding, the dream went belly-up. The car industry faltered. The wealth moved out. Crime and poverty moved in. The city's population more than halved in just twenty years. Even the music changed from major to minor – the biggest-selling recent Detroit star is Eminem, with his tales of the American underbelly and all that went with it. As the city's infrastructure fell apart, so did its ability to fund any kind of services for its citizens; and on 18 July 2013 the city of Detroit filed for bankruptcy, owing more than $18 billion.

The effect on those who lived there was personal and severe. Rates of depression soared. But, more often than not, doctors didn't see that journey down in their patients until a point at which it was very hard to get those patients back up.

Against that backdrop doctors at the Henry Ford Medical Center decided to try something different. And it was simple – to ask everyone who passed through their doors how they were feeling. Not in a cheesy tell-me-about-your-inner-soul kind of way, but in a very practical let's-get-rid-of-the-stigma way. Sounds so simple, doesn't it? And so, so effective, because what that means is that if you twist your ankle or burst an appendix or get whiplash in a car accident, when you go to see the doctor or nurse you'll be asked – in a very normal way – how your head is, too. Just by asking every patient who passed through the doors of a Henry Ford Medical Center straightforward questions about their mental health enabled people to give very straightforward answers. It put mental health in the same vein – and yes, I have said that deliberately – as taking your blood pressure or listening to your heart. One of the simple keys to it was that every patient knew that every other patient was being asked the same questions – so that taboo of feeling different, or difficult or ashamed was taken out of the equation.

And so people were able to say that they were feeling down, or had symptoms of anxiety or perhaps were experiencing far more severe episodes in a way that they hadn't done before. They didn't have to wait until things got so bad that they *had* to get to a doctor. The previously frighteningly high suicide levels had alerted doctors to the obvious fact that people simply weren't coming forward and self-identifying their mental health needs in time.

Not every suicide is preceded by a period of poor mental health either, which is why it was so important to look at the problem from all angles.

The zero element of the policy meant that the health provider wasn't thinking and budgeting for a certain amount of poor mental health based on what had happened in the last fiscal year; it was saying we need to look at every patient as being potentially at risk and budget for that in our services accordingly.

And if you consider that everyone is at risk, then you treat the insomnia, the mild anxiety, the continuous migraines, the drinking, diabetes, having a baby, whatever really, in a different way whereby you are also watching out for how mental health might be affected as well as physical wellbeing, and, most importantly of all, you are not signing off patients just when the physical problem gets better. It is an acceptance that simply being human puts you at risk.

Ten years into the project, the Henry Ford Medical group recorded zero suicides among its patients.

It is an interesting tale about the power of change. Of course, this is not the silver bullet or panacea for all mental-health problems, but I think it speaks to the relevance of your email. Because although the man with his beard and his crossed legs and the woman with her happy houseplants might be annoying with their 'wellness' agenda, just seeing something in a chemist while considering a haemorrhoid cream and/or buying yet another split-end-curing hair mask might enable the person who is just starting to go downhill to head to a place of safety before it all gets in too much of a tangle. And you are right: there do seem to be a lot of people in a tangle.

Like you, I am constantly amazed by the number of people in public life who now want to 'open up' about their mental vulnerability. It does seem to be a badge that has moved from the inside of the coat to the lapel. I don't doubt how difficult their experiences have been, or how hard it is to go public about something that you worry might affect your future employment opportunities, or be the first thing that people think of when they think of you. So, although largely sympathetic, I admit I have sometimes thought that it hasn't really held them back – which is both a good thing and a bad thing. Were I younger now – and not know my mind as well as I do – I could be forgiven for thinking that you can have huge social anxiety and panic attacks or depression and not leave your house for months at a time, but then suddenly find yourself beaming your way down the red carpet again positively enhanced by that miserable experience – as well as having gained millions more likes and follows from strangers on the Insta feed.

Getting through something is to be applauded, while enhancing a reputation? Mmmm, I don't know. I am not sure that message always helps. As you so correctly point out, mental-health conditions are often exacerbated and worsened by the environment you are in, so it might be fine for an A-list actress to get over her social phobias and depression and return to a life of fulfilment and ambition, but it's not that easy for most people, who might lose their jobs if they don't show up for weeks on end and certainly face at least a six-month wait to get an appointment at their local CAMS. I think I'd have more respect and sympathy if every star who showed their mental-health pants to the public also put some of the money from their next venture into building an 'I've Won a Bafta Psychiatric Wing for Severe Schizophrenia' at their local hospital. The stuff we are really still so scared to see and understand.

Which brings me to the serious point that you are making, too – there is a whole world of difference between mental wellness/mindfulness and really severe psychiatric illnesses. Many severe conditions are not curable, and only just treatable. Anyone who has watched a loved one suffer with the latter will probably agree that this clatter around temporary not-quite-wellness can also make people with real difficulties feel that if

only they could try a bit harder, or do yet another wellness class, or be more mindful with candles and rituals
or eat more brazil nuts or have more 'talking therapy',
then they would be able to help themselves. But they
simply can't – theirs are beautiful but excruciatingly
painful and different minds, which simply won't respond
to a series of online classes they can take with someone
called Erin in West California. Merchandising available.
If this cashmere-ensconced level of higher satisfaction
just seems ridiculous to me, God knows how it appears
to those who are just about clinging on. I do wish all that
lot would just shut up.

I write this as we emerge from a third pandemic lockdown. It is very obvious that the world will have millions
and millions of people struggling with mental-health
disorders caused by the pandemic and the extraordinary
stresses it has placed on so many.

There will be a massive rush to feel happy and joyful
and optimistic again. My fear is that this is an unrealistic
goal. We would do better to treat our re-emergence into
the world like a deep-sea diver approaching the surface.
Take our time, stay in the chilly bit just below for a while
before bursting out into the sunshine. I can't help feeling,
too, that for those with more severe problems the notion
that 'normal' has returned will make their own personal
space seem even harder to bear again.

So I'd say make more of those pamphlets. Send more
of those emails. Maybe lose the bloke sitting cross-legged
and the happy houseplant woman, though. Ask some

slightly more difficult questions, show some more realistic images of flats clogged up with a pandemic year's worth of misery and claustrophobia. And honestly, Jane, aspidistras as the sign of spinsterhood and sadness, you say? Cheeky. Mine went the same way as all my houseplants do. Shall we just say that if someone had just watered them, and misted them and cared for them a wee bit more in tiny amounts at the beginning of their demise, then perhaps they wouldn't have got to the critical stage, and then to the beyond-any-help-at-all stage.

See what I've done there? My apologies if it's stretched the metaphor a little too far, heads are not houseplants I know; but actually the 'small-steps-of-intervention approach' is probably exactly the same.

14

DID YOU PACK THAT BAG YOURSELF?:

DUTY FREE, SPEEDY BOARDING AND DOORS TO MANUAL

FI

TWO SUITCASES SIT IN my cupboard right now, like abandoned warehouses of dreams.

I imagine the extremely-average-quality plastic might creak a bit when I open them.

Inside there'll just be the wafting fluff from various 'easy-to-get-to' European destinations, although there is a possibility that they might also be where I put last year's re-giftable Xmas presents. Never mind. They'll keep.

As with all our luggage, these suitcases haven't gone anywhere for quite a while. They too have been furloughed. There's nothing special about them – I wheeled them noisily back from the local market a couple of years ago after realising that the previous incumbents wouldn't survive another outing in the bowels of a DC-10. I instantly regretted my purchase: there were a couple of zinging yellow ones, but for some reason I opted for boring black. This means my two suitcases are exactly the same as yours and everybody else's coming round the carousel.

It's a design flaw in a product whose key feature should be that it is instantly recognisable in a sea of similarity. Every year while jostling around the carousel, keening at the luggage hatch like a meerkat scenting the wind, I swear I'll fix this issue with some form of personalised stickerage, but every year I forget. And if you break down the holiday experience, it is exactly this kind of puzzling lack of logic, and ability to wipe stuff from the memory, that runs through it like a stick of rock.

Can we consider 'the suitcase' for a moment longer? In order to do this I need you to cast your mind back to what documentaries on BBC4 always refer to as 'a golden time' of travel – when a plane still felt properly glamorous, you were never going to actually *know* anyone who'd been to the Maldives and luggage didn't have wheels.

It seems extraordinary that there was once this time. And yes, I'm going to dwell on the wheels. In the 1970s we were travelling more than most five- and six-year-old kids on account of Dad working abroad. It wasn't my choice of a childhood but it was just what happened. I know I should remember something more exotic about the whole thing, but actually one of my abiding memories is of the struggle of luggage. Perhaps because I was so small and it was all so big, but at every airport people would be lugging these unfeasibly huge suitcases with them – straining every inch of their bodies to pull them up on to counters or lug them off in the direction of a trolley. Hernias popped out before people had even checked in. Marriages disintegrated before your very eyes as a universal cry of 'What on earth is in this thing, love?' echoed round Level 5 of all major airport car parks.

If you were heading off to start a new life or returning to an old one, I get it – but for a two-weeker on the Algarve that's a spot-on question. What on earth *is* in those suitcases? Why *do* people need so much stuff? But more importantly, how did it take so long for suitcase designers to realise the flaw? Why would you design a two-foot-by-one-foot suitcase capable of carrying 30 kilos of crap in it and not consider the fact that, when full, it is simply impossible to move?

And when the first little trolley cabin bags arrived did all the suitcase designers sigh in unison – 'Ahhhh, that's it. Wheels.'

It is one of so many things that make no sense about the thing that should make perfect sense – the vacation. A break from routine. A sojourn away from the norm. Time well spent and plenty of it, shared with the people you love the most, sometimes with plenty of them, too.

I strongly suspect that there is a crossroads in every woman's life where 'the holiday' goes from being adventurous, liberating, rejuvenating, or just nice to . . . er daunting, exhausting, and if I am honest – sometimes dreaded? I have probably done more than my fair share of travelling, not just because of a childhood spent traversing three continents in order to see a parent, but later in life for work. As the least important presenter on *The Travel Show* for several years in my twenties, I made mini-films in about thirty countries over the course of three series – politely reviewing mid-range hotels and experiences with the occasional leer at a palace or a 'place of interest'. I can tell you bite-sized pieces of information about where to go for a night out in Lisbon in 1996, and we once went up in a helicopter above the Victoria Falls with the doors removed 'to get a better shot'. I know. I can't quite believe we did that either. It was a glorious job. One that spoiled me. And perhaps, as a consequence, I've not been an adventurous holidaymaker as a parent. Actually, I'm really bad at it. I fantasise about creating some kind of a secret meeting place at airports – maybe by the oversized chocolate bars and universal chargers in WH Smiths – a place where like-minded mums could meet secretly and just make a run for it together to a decent Travelodge near Maidenhead for a week.

I wonder if it's a phase that passes – maybe when the kids have upped and left, when you start getting brochures for cruises the wrong way up the Danube, and when it might be quite exciting to go there with someone else's luggage? Possibly. But also possibly not. Read the room everyone, maybe we should have reined it in a while back.

Everything changed after 9/11 for good reason. I understand the need for heightened security, but none of it makes *logical* sense any more. When you are asked at the check-in desk, 'Did you pack the bag yourself?', how many ne-er-do-wells would ever say, 'No I left that to a dodgy-looking person whom I'd never met before who randomly asked if he/she could pack it for me.' Or if you are actually dealing with someone who has put something evil in their bag, if they answer yes they aren't lying, but you are no closer to being safe. In both those situations you haven't really weeded anyone out.

I also understand the need for physical security checks, and heaven knows I've been very grateful for the occasional firm pat-down at Brive la Gaillarde Airport – 'Gateway to the Dordogne', don't you know – but couldn't you add all the 100ml bottles together if you wanted to and then you'd have about a litre of whatever?

Once you have started to think like this, trust me, the whole experience becomes so mind-frazzlingly terrifying, you look so anxious and concerned that you are always the one they pick out for a 'random check', and that doesn't help. *And* we haven't even got through Duty Free yet.

Oh bloody hell. Duty Free. That's a land mass all of its own these days. It used to be a simple place of Benson & Hedges, large bottles of Gordon's gin and a couple of Chanel perfume stands. I had no idea I even *was* paying duty on giant bags of M&M's, large saucissons and 'I Heart London' T-shirts. A lot of thought has gone into how you pass through Duty Free now, with that bendy path that makes you walk in between the perfumes – which all end up smelling the same because there are so many of them.

It nods to the fact that everything about the travel experience has been designed to fleece you.

All I really need to say to you on this are two words: Speedy Boarding. No, did you? How embarrassing for you. Speedy Boarding is hilarious. It is like Nespresso shops – where the hopeful meet the damned. Where expectation at a high price is charged and where reality and all its disappointments are waiting for you. You are a lacklustre, environmentally dubious coffee pod in human form. More people are now in the Speedy Boarding queue than not, effing and blinding away as it dawns on them that it has not been £17.99 well spent. And because I have overthought the process of boarding a plane as well as every other aspect of the travel experience, I do have some suggestions . . . mainly wouldn't it make sense for everyone on the window seats to board first? Then the middle seat, and then the aisle? The time is taken up by all that unseemly jostling and 'You go in first, Oh sorry yes I am by the window, can I just scramble over you' etc. etc.

Then we get to on-board sales, the lottery cards, the delay taking off, the scramble to identify your big black suitcases in a carousel of copycats, the race for the car-hire stand before the entire plane descends on it and then the opportunity to initial here, here, here, here and here and here to agree to a scratched and smelly Ford Focus to power your way on a motorway for three hours in search of your lost rural idyll. The keyword there being 'lost'. I frequently am.

Yet the memory of all of this hassle fades, along with the creases marked into your knees by the seat in front of you and the very strange smell of the airline toilet, and by jiminy if you're not up late on Boxing Day next year booking another sojourn to Corfu, happily embracing the thirty minutes you'll spend being kettled in a stair-well with 200 passengers (non-speedy) before heading out across the hot tarmac to clamber into your tiny seat and wait to be offered the opportunity to buy a double gin and tonic with a 'Hot cheese melt' for twenty-eight euros. When would you *ever* think to pair those two items together? And why would you do it when you're strapped into a turbulence machine with only four work-ing toilets?

But give me this type of experience any day over that of The Explorer. You know the ones – they traverse hot deserts with only one camel and a TV crew for company. They go and plant flags at the top of mountains, despite the fact that they left a couple of toes at base camp and one lung at 2,000 feet. Men called Benedict or Kenneth or Ernest or Ranulph – can anyone name me an explor-ing Keith? They put the 'man' in Kathmandu. This is largely because no woman could be arsed. It's enough to get round Sainsburys on a wet Monday and stay sane, let alone make a food plan for the Himalayas.

For most of us, travel is about finding comfort and a restorative experience – the very idea that you'd be in-terested in reliving someone's attempts to take their own body to the edge of its ability to survive just seems weird. It runs counter to my inner desire and need to keep tiny things warm and alive. I would not want to experience the opposite sensation any more even if it came with 100,000 Avios points. Which leads me to points. Gosh, it was a genius who first thought those up. Sometimes all I do is look at how far away I could get WITH MY POINTS. I have never been interested in visiting either Ohio or Addis Ababa – but look, I've got enough points, and suddenly they are both in the running! I could fly to Greenland *one way in Business Class* with my points. How soon can we leave?! Or ten round trips to Aberdeen anyone? Come on, let's do it!

Except we can't at the moment. In the last year I've only left London twice. And there is a lot of me that is relieved. It comes with the very sincere caveat that lockdown life has not been so tough for us – I have stayed in work, we have a garden, the kids have got on with their schooling, Nancy the greyhound has been a fabulous get-out-of-the-house motivator, not least because her wind is so bad that there is no other option than to head out into the fresh air. I am not high on the list of people who have 'needed a holiday'.

I understand why we travel. It doesn't matter how uncomfortable or just rude all that experience is, we go back for more mainly because we like the notion of promise. Not the product, the promise. A far, far more potent thing. We tell ourselves that we need a break from the norm, from work, from drudge, from dull climates and boring jobs. We need to walk on sand, swim in the sea, see something different, be outside of ourselves. And we do need those things.

But, for the sake of the planet, we can't carry on yearning and indulging in something that is causing so much harm, can we? The old adage that travel broadens the mind is simply not true either. Travelling more has not cured xenophobia. Quite the opposite. The chance to witness more lives seems to have led to a greater distance between us all, not a closer bond. As much as we, in the privileged developed world, like to travel, we don't seem terribly happy to accept the notion that others might want to do the same thing, for far greater need and reason than just taking a break from the norm and giving our nice kaftans an annual waft.

Sometimes the scales fall from your eyes, don't they? Should what has happened in the big, wide world change our habits in our tiny personal worlds? Haven't our tiny worlds been hinting at a massive gap between expectation and reality for a while now? And that is a genuine question. I'd like the answer in your very best captain's voice please, Garvey. The one with authority, purpose and definitely a landing slot at Heathrow Terminal 5. Not the tired, gloomy, pissed-off late-night Luton one. It's always a bit of a worry when that one comes across the tannoy. I've added it to the list.

JANE

'AND THE PILOT **WAS A WOMAN**!!' Many a 1970s and 1980s holiday got off to a jittery start for Nigel in

49C when she came over the intercom. You can imagine the eulogy at his passing: 'Nigel was a loyal friend, a lifelong misogynist, a keen supporter of Cloggers FC, and a dedicated Speedy Boarder.' Don't worry, Nige, I know my limits when it comes to aircraft and I think, realistically, co-pilot might be about it. Obviously, I'd like to do all the announcements.

It's a tough one, travel. We know our own economy needs a thriving tourist industry; we know some other countries near and far are now dependent on foreign tourism; and we know cutting carbon emissions is vital. During the third lockdown in early 2021, the national conversation in Britain shifted, suddenly, to The Holiday. It was our human right to wish and plan for one; it was simultaneously selfish beyond reason to even consider such a thing when some people had been trapped in their homes for almost a year. I found myself on both sides of the argument, most of the time. As usual.

As Fi says, it's not as if holidays were even that easy. Airports are certainly no longer a carefree gateway to the tropics; they seethe with tension, mile-long queues, mile-wide men with machine guns, ever-changing rules and then, your hulking black suitcase taking its own chances, you find yourself in a high-end shopping mall, Clarins rather suddenly laid before you. And there you inexplicably spend a lot of money on a body lotion.

Once on board, you glance in what you hope is a sisterly and supportive fashion at the poor lone woman with a small baby and a toddler making her way down the aisle, praying fervently they're sitting at least thirty rows away. You're pointlessly irritated by the man in tasselled shoes reading the *Financial Times*. He's utterly indispensable at the office and can hardly believe he's going on holiday at all, really. In fact he might have to fly home early. God, he hopes so. And so do the rest of his family, on the quiet.

Now just relax, sit back, obviously panic a bit about whether you can remember where the whistle is on the life jacket, should you land in water, and prepare for take-off. It'll soon be time to cough up for a very cold M&S ploughman's sandwich and a small tin of Diet Coke. This is the life!

Like Fi, I have chosen to put myself through this very gentle version of hell on an annual basis.

Deep down, I believe I deserve a holiday, a 'break'. I also know this is nonsense. There is nothing more jarring than the middle-class bleat of entitlement. Of course I'd like one – I fancy not cooking and limiting my options to a choice between the new Jane Harper or the latest Robert Harris, with an occasional break to reapply the factor 50 and be roundly mocked by my companions for my pale-skinned caution. I'm ashamed to say I do not care much for ruins. A good rummage around a local market is fine, as long as it's over way before noon. And what I emphatically don't want is what many women are still served up as a 'holiday': the chance to do exactly what they do at home, except in a more confined space and with fewer utensils.

Still, for someone from the drizzly British Isles, nothing beats the simple certainty of daily sunshine. I didn't go abroad at all until I was nearly sixteen, and that was a German exchange trip. I don't remember the weather; I do remember my pen pal's dad wearing a roomy cotton vest at the breakfast table. There were gasps in genteel suburban Liverpool when I mentioned this on my return. My grandmother, in particular, was horrified. She had never been abroad, unless you counted Ireland, which she didn't. And this was confirmation that it was simple folly. Why would you put yourself through all the stress, only to be confronted by a plate of salami before 8 a.m. and a chubby chap in his underwear?

The Garveys were not travellers. The world was explored on our behalf, largely by men who'd been to spartan boarding schools and owned khaki shorts with pockets, thus equipping them to explain the planet to the rest of us.

For us it was seaside Britain all the way. And I loved it, mostly. The crinkle of sand between the toes, the raspberry sauce trickling down your 99. I've had Hawaiian Tropic generously and, let's face it, optimistically, applied in Abersoch, Gwynedd. I've had milk poured on to the raging sunburn on my almost blue, mole-y thighs. It's not easy to pull off bright-red thighs in a hot-pink one-piece, and with the faint whiff of cheese, but I like to think I made a reasonable job of it.

Speaking for everyone who sat in a slate-museum car park in North Wales as a child, waiting for the clouds to part, eager to pounce on any scrap of good news on the weather front – 'Look! There's enough blue sky now to make an elephant a pair of underpants!' – we never get over the thrill of not just hoping for sunshine tomorrow, but waking first thing in the morning and knowing it will be there. I dare say tantric sex *is* great, but dear old Sting would have to revisit the form of his life to beat the bagging-the-sunbed shift: early-morning rays by the hotel pool in Crete, first cuppa on the go (you remembered your proper tea bags, of course) and the prospect of the breakfast buffet still to come. You know the one, you fill up so you don't 'need' lunch, then go on to have lunch anyway.

A selection of cold meats. Two slices of mild cheese. A chunk of cucumber and five tomatoes. No bread. Well, maybe a small roll. And they really are only small, and locally made by artisans, so probably two of those. And sometimes these places do pancakes. Chocolate sauce? Well, you are on holiday. So why not?

You see? You're transported. I'll be back. I bet you will be too. Doors, emphatically, to manual.

15

HAPPY BLOODY CHRISTMAS:

TURKEY CROWNS AND DECEMBER FRAZZLE

JANE

CHRISTMAS ALWAYS STARTS FOR ME with the arrival of The Card, the one addressed to me in the married name I never used, even when I was married. Every year, I tell myself this is nothing, merely the wearying affectation of an Older Person, and I should pay no heed. And every year, I fail to self-soothe and develop a knot of tension in my neck. Here it is again. It's that time of year.

Of course, Christmas is also a hereditary disease – it passes down the maternal line. The teenage girl who was once so dismissive of her mother's December frazzle ('What IS the matter with her?') may, decades later, find herself helplessly gripped by the same seasonal fervour. Powerless, apparently, to stop herself doing too much, for too many, for very little recognition.

Women do Christmas. We make it; we maintain it. Increasingly, we complain about it. But nothing changes, and I suspect we wouldn't really want it to.

It creeps up on you, the December frazzle. One year you're just an adolescent bystander, the recalcitrant, shiny-faced attendee, a sophisticate-in-training who mocks the bottles of Mateus Rosé and Black Tower; the next, you're red-faced in your own kitchen in a novelty pinny, and everyone's turning to you and asking about the bread sauce, the bin bags and the chance of a spare towel. These are responsibilities you never wanted. You deeply resent them, the absurdities and pettiness, and the sheer, unending REMEMBERING. All the stuff we now know to be 'emotional labour'. The cards for old family friends, presents for teachers, setting the alarm so you can tip the bin men. I once tweeted about the latter, and a wag snapped: 'I've got a tip for your bin men. Don't be bin men.' The wag was an idiot. Tip your bin men.

Everyone likes to think they have quaint family traditions. In the land of the 1970s, strange customs also prevailed. A neighbour would visit on Christmas morning with presents for my sister and me. We were teenage girls; he was, I suppose, well into his forties. And he always bought us knickers. We would take them, summon up the acceptable amount of polite simpering, and then dash off, eyes rolling. This relatively benign incident is wonderfully illustrative of 'a different time' – that catch-all phrase used to excuse much of what was considered perfectly normal in that decade, and now strikes most of us, frankly, as just a trifle weird.

We'd always squeeze in a huge row, too, usually, though not necessarily, on Boxing Day. That was the day my parents always had a 'Drinks', which meant domestic tension hung in the air from the watery first light, the passive-aggressive hoovering was well under way by 9 a.m., and my sister and I would be dragged from our beds and set to work, filling the nibbles bowls. We would be expected to 'look smart' (No Jeans or Trainers) and be entertained by people we dismissed as middle-aged bores, always asking us what 'our plans' were. By 2.30 p.m. the central heating would be going fit to burst and groups of avuncular, red-faced men in V-necked sweaters and terrible shoes were bound to be debating law and order. The country was well and truly going to the dogs, and yes, go on then, I'll have another one IF YOU INSIST! My sister and I knew then that it was only a matter of time before someone called for the return of National Service. At 7.45 p.m., as tasteless cheese-ball crumbs littered the carpet, the stragglers would be shown the door and my mother would make her annual vow NEVER to do that again.

To be fair, she must have been tired by then. Somehow, it was always up to her to cater for the wider family on 'the big day', and we had plenty of elderly folk who needed feeding. Some I liked more than others. One cocksure, Yorkshire-born great-aunt-by-marriage infuriated me one year by loudly insisting the 'Lonely Goatherd' puppet scene in *The Sound of Music* had been artfully inserted 'just for the telly'. I knew this was utter nonsense, but the old bird would not be shifted. I made my feelings on the issue clear and received a reprimand. I could've cheerfully bopped her on the head with the silver-effect After Eight trolley.

In adult life, I vowed, I was going to do things differently. There was simply no need for a martyr-ish approach. I would not be that woman, Old Mother Christmas, who flops on to the sofa last thing at night and is then asked where the scissors are, and cries 'I've ONLY JUST sat down!' before staggering to her feet to get them. Oh no. Not me, the person who could see the 'festive' season for what it was – a capitalist, patriarchal construct I would have no part of. Frankly, you could stick your giblet gravy where the sun don't shine. And as for the relatively recent fetishisation of small sausages wrapped in slivers of bacon, do me a favour. If they're so good, why don't we fold a rasher round a chipolata the rest of the year? And while I'm here, they never sell out. I have bought the perishing things in a leading high-street store at 5.25 p.m. on Christmas Eve. And they're going for a song on the 27th, if you're at all interested.

But I digress. Oh, I was full of good festive intentions. And it was easy to maintain a faint sense of disdain about the horror of it all before I became a parent. Yes, that does change things a bit.

I'm sure you don't need me to tell you this, but: unprotected sex in late-ish March may result in a Christmas baby. At least, it did for me.

So there I was, careful to stuff a couple of paperbacks in the maternity bag in the dying weeks of the twentieth century. I hadn't chosen anything too demanding, just a couple of thrillers I could get stuck into while the baby was . . . while the baby was . . . sleeping, was it? I wasn't that sure. But I imagined that sleeping probably came into it at some point.

The Millennium Bug (a potential computer glitch that threatened civilisation as we knew it) was a source of minor concern, rumbling away in the distance – I think the BBC had ordered a few more boxes of cornflakes CAMS for the bunker, let's put it that way – but we'd just stocked up with loads of bottled water, as advised. That was sensible, but did make it difficult to move up and down the very cramped hall of our very small ter-raced house. That was already hard enough for me, as my pregnancy had been entirely powered by carbs. I still think fondly of the slab of apple pie I'd treat myself to from our local coffee shop. It was organic, you see, so hardly counted. And it contained fruit. There are willowy goddesses with exquisitely neat 'baby bumps' – women who look like they might have inadvertently eaten a bite-size pork pie they mistook for a mushroom – and then there are five-foot-one-inch Weebles, who at thirty-eight weeks' gestation can barely stay upright, after months hurling themselves at every form of baked good going. I'd certainly been eating for two – as long as the baby emerged fully adult-sized, and possibly in the form of an Olympic shot-putter called Igor. In the event, she was a rather delicate seven pounds seven ounces. I'm proud to say that, two decades later, I have 'shed my baby weight' and can regularly be seen flaunting my curvy figure in loose-fitting tracksuit bottoms.

I had high hopes for the whole experience. It was a naivety borne entirely out of my own good fortune. I wasn't young – thirty-four, for Pete's sake, geriatric first-time mother territory – but people had always been pretty nice to me so far. And in my professional life as a radio presenter, of course, great dollops of praise and affirmation were bestowed upon me quite routinely. Frankly, it was one of the reasons I did it. I could do my job, just DO it, and someone would give me a version of 'You were marvellous, darling.' I mean this was *Drive-time* on BBC Radio Five Live, not *Hedda Gabler* at the Old Vic, but you get my drift.

Childbirth, though, this was different. And extra-ordinary. I was surely deserving of a truckload of bouquets. This was a lot harder than asking a taciturn grandad from Grimsby why he was so determined to make a model of the Ark Royal out of matchsticks, or handing crisply over to the traffic 'n' travel desk. I had produced another human being, albeit a tiny one, from my very person, just minutes after I'd waddled into the operating theatre with as much dignity as I could muster in the flapping NHS gown, a mere four and a bit stone heavier than what might have been called my fighting weight.

All this pre-C-section chat about it feeling like some-one's doing the washing-up in your stomach. Nonsense. I didn't feel much at all, and certainly not pain, but I did sense a man with surprisingly hairy arms (is this a fan-tasy? Possibly. But who fantasises about stuff like this?)

tugging a slightly resistant baby human from my belly as 'God Rest Ye Merry Gentlemen' spluttered tinnily from a cassette player. Congratulations to me.

Now here's what should happen next – you should be transported, on cloud nine, to a place of peace and sanctuary. You should be allowed a choice of all your favourite foods. Go on, have a ruddy great wedge of Brie, woman – you can now! Wood nymphs should circle the bed, dance a celebratory jig for you and then mop your brow with something silken; perhaps your mother could pop in for a minute or two, as long as she doesn't say anything irritating.

What actually happens is that the magic spell is soon broken – your NHS smock is wrenched down with little or no ceremony, and you, a professional woman who has asked searching questions of Members of Parliament and has been thought moderately witty on occasion, are exposing your less-than-perky breasts to all and sundry. Someone (you're not sure who) calls you 'Mummy' and you think God help them, they've lost their tiny mind.

Five days later, after all-night feeding battles and an opportunity to help decorate the ward's Christmas tree one-handed, we are free to leave. It is 23 December.

Yes. And there's no time to waste. Unbelievably, the whole family are COMING FOR CHRISTMAS. Who made that decision, and why, is forever lost in the fug of confusion that surrounds this time. Perhaps just as well. There's no doubt about the highlights. I am constipated (not uncommon after copious painkillers, of course), and my dad is dispensed to find an emergency chemist for a laxative on Christmas morning. He does not know London, satnav is not yet invented, and my bowels are now the sole topic of debate for two families and four generations, if you include the baby. Ding-dong merrily to you, too. Not only am I almost permanently bare-chested while people who know nothing about it offer me breast-feeding advice, but my most basic bodily functions are now being discussed by all and sundry. Ever fancied being a woman of mystery, an enigma? Now, love, is not the time.

On Christmas afternoon, after the usual absurdly complicated festive lunch (again – WHY??), my sister and I retreat upstairs to try out the breast pump. We're a long way from trying to see if we could get the radio tuned to Radio Luxembourg. But if I could get the sodding contraption to work, then maybe, maybe, I might be able to sleep for more than ninety minutes at a stretch. Sadly, we are both as clueless and incapable as each other. I can barely produce a trickle of nature's finest, and I do not enjoy the sensation of being milked like a less-than-prizewinning Jersey cow, BY MY OWN SISTER. I should say at this point there's no evidence she was having the time of her life either.

Even then, I think I knew I'd find this funny one day. And perhaps one night when your adolescent off-spring have wound you up, lurching from an Uber at who-knows-what-o'clock, you could get your revenge by revisiting their early days, barging into their rooms uninvited, offering milk or a comforting cuddle whenever it took your fancy. See how they like it now.

No Christmas has ever been quite that fraught again, unless you count the one I spent mostly in the cellar drinking and texting, or the Norovirus one. We don't need to go into detail on that – you may well have experienced something similar yourself. Just think virulent tummy bug, blue cheese and a packed inter-generational household. Still, I can never go into my magnificent corner shop without recalling my visit on that fateful Boxing Day afternoon when I strode in, Boudicca in her pomp, and asked for a fresh mop head and a bottle of Dettol. And please be quick about it, my good man. He didn't blink. He never does: you could go in there and ask for a nuclear warhead and some small brown envelopes and the reaction would be exactly the same.

The Christmas of 2020 couldn't happen. No one actually said the pandemic would all be over by Christmas, but I suppose I assumed it would be. The tree would arrive and be decorated and I would absolutely love it, and by the 28th I'd be asking why Queen Victoria's choice of husband had led to perfectly sane human beings bringing trees into their houses decades later, shedding needles everywhere and acting as a sort of Wacky Warehouse for hyperactive kittens.

We would all be together, and we'd try especially hard because the year had been so challenging; someone would inevitably say something that was bound to upset someone else; Dad would say how he always forgot how terrible it was to have a day without a newspaper; I would be stressed and resentful, as is my right every year. And then history is briskly rewritten, and everyone agrees they had a lovely time and yes, we ate at 2 p.m. this year, what about you?

But no – it was just the three of us. It had to be. No stress, nothing to feel resentful about. Mother and daughters cobbled up a lunch, a mixture of ready-made side dishes, a tiny turkey crown and a vegan's innovative ways with sprouts. Roast them, bit of balsamic glaze. They were delicious. We all tried a teaspoon full of an individual M&S Plant Kitchen Christmas pud to show willing. We watched *Love Actually* and hated it, all over again. And only the next morning I realised how genuinely, gently memorable it had been. None of us will ever forget this one. Just us. Unlikely to be repeated – and in many ways, I hope it isn't.

It's an irresistible force, the festive season – not just the baubles, the stars, the flashing Santas, all the bright lights and flickering flames we deploy to fight off the winter blues. It's the faint hope and the promise of something better. Perhaps we really can be kinder. Perhaps we were actually better all along. Perhaps next Christmas . . .

FI

WELL, I SUPPOSE AT the heart of every Christmas there is a birthing story . . . but Good Lord. What *on earth* is going on here? This is like playing inverse Christmas Present Face – you know the one, the fixed smile of appreciation, the dubious yelp of excitement – or is it a real yelp? To be so involved with Christmas and take the time to loathe it so much . . . I feel it might be a sign that you do rather like all the hassle after all. But maybe you properly don't, and I need to stage an intervention.

If I am staging an intervention, then it is simply this:

To you, Jane, and every woman who 'may find herself helplessly gripped by the same seasonal fervour. Powerless, apparently, to stop herself 'doing too much, for too many, for very little recognition' can I just say please *do* stop. Just that. You have a duty to your two daughters to accept some form of treatment in order to prevent transmission of this terrible disease. For goodness' sake, one of them has a birthday to deal with, too! Don't pass on to her the mantle of out-of-proportion panic that sets in when you realise that there isn't a vegan 'it's-not-a-pig-and-it's-not-a-blanket-either' left to be found in East West Kensington. It really doesn't matter; they are available all year round in Dalston. Come on over. Spend Christmas with us, where you can sing carols while the microwave merrily pings in time in the background, gently reheating large parts of the Christmas lunch thoughtfully made by a variety of local supermarkets and simply bought online (booked back in November, admittedly). I'll wrap a sausage in a piece of bacon just for you if you need me to.

But do you know what overwhelming message I take

from this? It is your point that it's best not to have any form of romantic contact in March. You are bang on the money there. It may well feel like spring in your heart, but in December it will feel like an almighty melon in your wotsit.

16

THE CHUFF OF LIFE:

SIGNATURE DISHES AND
MOISTURISING REGIMES

FI

OBVIOUSLY, I WANTED TO include a chapter about how I owe everything in life to my studiously acquired knowledge of the early works of Sophocles and Plato. I know you'd have thoughts on that too, Jane, and I am sorry if my failure to share these insights disappoints. But as I think we both agree that a chortle is as good for levelling the mind as any attempt at understanding *The Republic*, here's a list of questions for you, Garvey, which I have attempted to answer too. They are just about the chuff of life. And by chuff I mean the bits that hang around in the corner of life's drawer that we all seem to have. The dust around the edges. You once asked what the stuff was in the cutlery drawer and how it got there. The bits and pieces. The tiny gritty bits. Looks like salt and pepper but isn't. And this is how 'Cutlery Chuff' was born. It's this kind of tiny but universal observation that makes a Garv a Garv, so here it is on a grander scale. It's not the stuff of life, it is the chuff of life. Do your very worst with them.

I have also turned your Statutory Questions, on signature dishes and moisturising regimes, back atcha. About bloody time.

1. *If you were in a witness protection scheme, who would your new identity be and what would your life be like?*

Fi: I'd be a hairdresser, and I'd quite like to live on the coast. This is presumably a good combination because the inclement elements will mean a very busy salon. I'd make the most of the enormous police budget (I've been ever so brave in coming forward and ratting on the perps, so I've got gold-star treatment) and have some plastic surgery to alter my appearance. Probably a couple of inches on my tibia, and definitely a little lift around the eyes. I'd have to change my voice a bit – and so would you, it's turned out to be quite a recognisable thing about us. I think I'll go broad Yorkshire and I'll affect the short 'a's you so often take the piss out of me for not currently using. In terms of the other basics, I'd like to be called Barbara and have three dogs – small, medium and large.

Jane: Let's take a moment to ponder this woman's chances (or, as she would say, charnces) of maintaining a convincing Yorkshire accent. I think there'll be widespread mirth from Bingley to Mytholmroyd at the thought of that. I'm not even certain she could handle three dogs, based on her current greyhound Nancy's lackadaisical relationship with discipline. As for hairdressing, that's not something I'd trust to an amateur, not even a brave one in hiding. But yes, OK, that's your fantasy, Barbara. No, I don't want any product.

As for me, I'd get a job on the oil rigs. Well, all right, that's the answer my handlers have told me to give. The truth is, I've been deep, deep undercover for the best part of half a century. And you've got to say it was working pretty well until my ego got the better of me just then.

2. *What's the mantra that rings true to you, and the one that really doesn't?*

Jane: 'If at first you don't succeed, try, try again.'

This is a spot-on mantra and one I apply regularly to reversing into a tight space. I sometimes do it brilliantly and without effort on the very first go, always, without fail, unwitnessed by a single living soul. But if anyone's passing, and even if the gap is big enough for an Eddie Stobart, I'll fall to pieces. Yes, this is a shocking and sexist cliché. Sorry.

Also, home printers. Sometimes, on the eleventh attempt, when you can be on the brink of tears, the clunking heap of crap starts working again. Me neither.

'Nothing of real value ever comes easy' – now that's clearly nonsense. Go out, buy a reasonably priced dough-nut, stick the kettle on, sit down. You've earned it. You can always follow up with a bit of cucumber if you sense a bout of self-loathing coming on.

Fi: The one that really doesn't do it for me is 'Feel the Fear and Do It Anyway'. Why? Why, Jane? Why would centuries of evolution have enabled your body and mind to tell you something is dangerous only for you to override these innate fears in the hope of 'pushing your boundaries' or 'challenging your personal growth', or whatever sub-logical series of pseudo words have been put together to form an instantly appealing sentence for a Sunday supplement this week? 'Feel the Fear and Retreat Very Slowly and Stay In Your Comfort Zone' is much better I think.

The one that does mean the most and has always worked for me is 'To Thine Own Self Be True'. This is also available as 'Know Thyself' or 'Just Be Yourself'. Buy one, get two free! Your world is not anyone else's and you'd be a fool to live it by someone else's rules.

3. *What is your signature dish?*

Jane: These days I can provide hearty fare for vegans and vegetarians and I've learned a thing or two along the meat-free way: mashed potato is actively improved by Flora; coconut milk is very sweet and can be quite overwhelming; you can't beat beans. Borlotti, butter and cannellini are the unsung ones. But let's be honest: if I'm on my own I get a fresh loaf, eat the crust with a load of butter as a starter, then eat most of the rest with pâté or the strongest Cheddar I can get hold of. I know it's not a 'dish', as such.

Fi: My kitchen life changed when I got a deep-fat fryer – I'm not saying that we have tried putting everything in it . . . but . . . we pretty much have, and now I'm living a lot of my life in search of the perfect chicken schnitzel. Well, at least until the teens turn veggie. Which is when I will come looking for you.

4. *Moisturising regime?*

Fi: Never the same from one week to the next, I'm afraid. Some weeks almost none. Others a complicated cleansing-toning-moisturising regime that needs to begin at sunrise in order to be completed in time for bed. And you can't tell which week is which. Go figure, you silly massive beauty industry.

Jane: OK, Fi's got this one. I have spent £2.99 on moisturiser; I have spent a sum of money I truly can't bring myself to reveal on moisturiser; and at neither time did *anyone* comment on either my revitalised dewy freshness or my haggard, weather-beaten countenance. We are mugs. And you know what? I'll be a mug again.

5. *Would your life have been better had you been born a man?*

Jane: Seriously, I'd have loved a taste of the freedom most of them don't even know they have. To run, or walk, or just be, without judgement or fear. To sit in a pub with a pint doing the crossword on my own. To stand with my legs apart in paint-stained tracksuit bottoms and scratch my beard and say, 'It's going to cost you.'

Fi: Well, I guess in terms of money and job, prob-ably, but in terms of where I have ended up and levels of something approaching contentment-on-a-good-day

. . . no, absolutely not. Aside from astonishingly scary levels of poor mental health in men, the banter isn't as nourishing. And the role models are rubbish.

6. *If your eccentricity was ever backed up by a lottery win, how would it manifest itself?*

Jane: I've already had this conversation with myself, which is odd, because I don't do the lottery. My unlikely win would be enormous – the biggest rollover of them all – and I'd set up a charitable foundation in my name but be very careful not to talk too much about everything I do for charity.

Fi: Aren't you nice? I haven't got past the fantasy of being able to have a massive hot tub in the back garden. Surrounded by wafting high grasses. With a drinks fridge beside it. Stocked only with rather cheap but plaque-removingly dry Cava. I know – classy . . . how soon can you get here?

7. *In the warm conservatory of the BBC Retirement Home for the Impartial and Infirm, you have the row of chairs facing the sea. Just four chairs. Who occupy the three others?*

Jane: The thought of seeing out my dotage in the company of other retired egomaniacs is unnerving. But if pushed, I'll have the Blue Peter tortoise, Cilla Black and Dave Allen.

Fi: Alan Rusbridger, Joan Bakewell and Julie Walters.

8. *If you could create a new Farrow & Ball colour name what would it be?*

Jane: Flat White (of course).

Fi: Furlough – a dull grey with hints of blue.

9. *New business you could run based purely on the title?*

Jane: Heaven Scent – tiny bottles of perfume samples delivered every month; or Dead Honest – a service that offered warts-and-all, but largely affectionate, eulogies to be read at funerals.

Fi: Peas Be With You – a frozen-veg delivery service.

10. *Three words on the headstone?*

Jane: Nice but dull (see above).

Fi: Milked every opportunity or Annoyed Jane Garvey. Can't decide.

17

UNFORTUNATELY:

THE PODCAST NO ONE WANTED UNTIL IT STARTED TO DO QUITE WELL

JANE

DO A PODCAST, THEY SAID. I wasn't keen. I was in the grip of my lifelong curse, a self-defeating but persistent combination of laziness and arrogance. Despite not knowing what they were, I'd already decided podcasts definitely weren't for me.

PODCAST: 'an episodic series of spoken-word digital audio files that a user can download to a personal device for easy listening'. About as sensual a prospect as a turn around the park at dusk with a committed fan of George Formby. No, no thanks. I couldn't see the point. I'd made my mind up, until I changed it.

You could do it with Fi Glover, they said. Who? Why? I mean, what on earth . . . I knew the woman. I liked her. But I was also more than a trifle wary. There was a polished cleverness about her. She was witty, sophisticated and worldly, not world-weary, like me. I knew she was no stranger to a discreet booth at a private members' club while, I make no bones about it, I love the meatballs at Ikea. We were very different. Although it's true some senior management figures couldn't tell us apart. I don't know which one of us was most offended. OK, I do.

Anyway, the Fates intervened, in the form of an assertive senior producer with an impressive moustache. A man, as it happens. Before I could think of an excuse, I was locked in a studio with old Ms Wet-look Catsuit and told to talk. The horrific results of our first pod-date are in a high-security vault deep underground, guarded by giant lizards. Dire, unusable, indulgent tosh (yes, I know people still say that now). We went ahead anyway.

We were outliers of a sort back then, or box-tickers, maybe. I know we haven't ticked many diversity boxes in our professional lives, so this was a bit of a novelty. When we began *Fortunately*, podcasts were thought of as the natural home of the freewheeling male, not a medium in which two middle-aged women could laugh at their own jokes, make disgraceful sexual references, or talk about their pets' flatulence. But here we are.

A glance at the list of the most successful podcasts tells you two women in their fifties are certainly not the norm. There are plenty of bantering comedy men; the full range of football chat, from knockabout to niche; a sprinkling of healthy living and the inspirational, and, of course, an abundance of true crime, with a lavish helping of serial killers. That old standby. Find me the medium that doesn't lend itself well to a serial killer, I beg of you.

We started slowly, and rather earnestly. There was a format, of sorts. Fi and I were to act as a kind of distracted woman's guide to the wonders of Radio 4, introducing short clips of 'content' we'd enjoyed. We sat perched on stools in a café overlooking the main BBC newsroom, enthused dutifully about a documentary on the French horn that hadn't had the attention it deserved, and tried not to be distracted by members of the public browsing the corporate memorabilia in the BBC gift shop. I'll have a Tardis keyring and a full-colour postcard of that lovely Matt Baker, please. It was all very free-form, sweary and loose, light years away from the structured world of British broadcasting where presenters really do have scripts that say, 'Well, it's that time of year again, when our thoughts turn to cobnuts . . .'.

Or maybe that was just me.

Gradually, we got better. My sister said *Fortunately* was an improvement on my broadcasting persona. Well, I think she actually said, 'You don't sound quite as much of a knob.' The original 'content' format was quietly forgotten when it emerged that the very few people listening at the time liked our rambling, inconsequential exchanges much more than the rather laboured hints to consume even more of the corporation's output.

In the summer, we'd move out to record the podcast in the ghastly concrete splendour of the BBC's piazza, attempting to grab a much-prized table outside Café Nero and hurling abuse and encouragement at the assorted egos striding by. Some were much more receptive than others. Clare Balding sat down for a chat and gave us the world exclusive that she and her wife Alice Arnold are entirely dependent on upmarket ready meals; David Dimbleby offered up a bit of his trademark, statesman-like twinkle; Huw Edwards remains, as I type, tantalisingly just out of reach . . . but perhaps our podcast encounter with the Welsh wizard of news should stay a delicious fantasy forever. It might be better all round.

Somewhere along the way, our podcast conversations became much more wide-ranging. And then our producers really started to save us from ourselves, delicately pruning some potentially career-ending references to ex-partners and past indiscretions. We cannot thank them enough. But in real life, women talk like this all the time, clashing world events with domestic trivia and personal confidences. We're often told men don't communicate with each other in the same way, but how would I know? Surely no one asks a friend to pop round for a solid, serious chat, and then has exactly that with no deviation from the script? Even in the most desperate of circumstances you'll find yourself veering off into an acknowledgement that someone's partner does indeed have halitosis, or someone else has bought terrible but expensive curtains. It's all grist to life's conversational mill. We all know the small stuff enables the big stuff to get said.

Fortunately became, stealthily, a moderate success. There was no clever marketing campaign or 'push', this was word-of-mouth, and fairly incessant tweeting from us. Which must have been boring, so sorry. For the first time in my working life, strangers came up to me in the street and on the Underground to talk about something I'd done. Some were very much like us – the middle-aged woman who often feels she's doing everything for everybody, with nobody taking any notice.

But it turned out we were attracting other listeners too, drawn in, apparently, by our 'authenticity'. I'm never entirely sure what that means. And let's be clear, we're talking about two people who've talked for a living for decades, talking to each other for money (that's Fi's phrase, heartbreaking isn't it?), and with a talented colleague holding a microphone and editing out the bad bits. So it's authentic, yes, up to a point. But what we weren't doing was pretending to be permanently riding the crest of a good time. I began to realise that this was a place where I could say I felt pretty miserable, if that was indeed how I felt. My genuine, unexpected and – yes – absurd grief at the dignified death of our family pet Mittens, a cat I hadn't even realised I liked, touched a nerve. Fi got the flu (remember the flu?) and I went round to see her with a bunch of tulips I'd bought at the Tube station, and we recorded the conversation. She sounded ill, because she was, and I started off sympathetic, at least, before reverting to type and making barbed remarks about her kitchen units.

Look, this really doesn't bear close analysis – no, I don't really know how we built an audience either.

And then there was Covid. We were banished from the piazza. Sent home to make the best of it along with all the other non-essential workers, and we kept the podcast going. Fi was much more technically accomplished, but I'd had years of being infantilised as a presenter, never allowed to touch anything sharp, and this meant I now had to learn some new skills, or at least skills that were very new to me. The history of this period has yet to be written, but I hope there's room to acknowledge the fate of the hapless chump, cast adrift from expert assistance, varifocals steaming up, hunched over a laptop and frantically googling 'How do I . . . ?'

Thanks to everyone who talked me through it all. I hope you felt it was worth it. Thanks to them, the podcast chuntered on, through lockdowns and tiers, bog-roll banditry and banana bread.

Over to you then, Fi. She said, in an entirely natural and unscripted way.

FI

THANK YOU, Jane.
(Pause)
My colleague Jane Garvey there.
(Pause)
Jane Garvey is the BBC Difficult Woman Correspondent.
(Pause)

Why do they do that on the TV news? We know who it was because the screen told us who it was, and the anchor had told us who it was at the start of the item and the item was only three minutes long and how much thanks does anyone need for doing their job anyway?

This is just one of the many things you don't have to do in a podcast.

For those of us who love the medium of radio the podcast thing has been ridiculously exciting. I do really mean that. To compensate for Garvey's world-weariness, I give you my breathless enthusiasm. Podcasting is radio without the support garments – and it's liberating, wobbling and joyful. There is no script. There is no real shape or form to it. There is no 'run-through'. You don't have to walk a producer through a set of questions. They don't have to walk you back. There is no real remit about the guests we have on. Anyone around the world can listen to it, and at a time of their choosing. A man called Vernon listens on the Costa del BBC Retirement. Beth is over in Hong Kong. Cher (not that one) is a regular from the USA. Our call-out for our longest-range listener once took us as far as the Himalayas.

Lots of people seem to like listening while out for a run. Although all of us who work in the medium might like to think that it is the sheer power of our content that makes audio so popular, the key is in the fact you can be doing something else at the same time. We simply brighten up a boring chore, distract from a dull run – or, judging by our email inbox – help endless people get to sleep. Not a prob . . . Oh look, you've gone already.

The only real thing wrong with old-fashioned radio was that you actually had to hear it. That sentence is not as daft as it might seem. One of radio's most appealing features – being live – was also one of its biggest weaknesses. If you didn't catch it in the moment, you could never get it back. And you couldn't decide when you wanted to listen to a programme, you had to wait for the station to decide for you. You could – if you really wanted to – record radio on to cassette tapes. One day *Antiques Roadshow* will have a special section for fifty-somethings to bring along their TDKs – you'll get a lot of money for the ones that didn't cut off 'Come on Eileen' halfway through at the end of the chart show.

With radio you were always in the thrall of the daily schedule. But, as soon as you could download bits and bobs on to a phone, podcasting was guaranteed to take off. And as soon as high-quality headphones became a thing – Beats' deal with Apple was worth $3.2 billion (note to Merchandising please, cc. Jane in, maybe this instead of the tea towels?) – audio achieved an ultimate intimacy that no other medium could. It literally gets inside your head. And of course that changes the style of what you want to hear. That formal programming, the clunk of the links and the restrictions of the running order – well, that is fine dining. That's when the radio is literally quite a long way away from you. Podcasting is the all-day diner – it offers something for everyone, whenever they want it – and in return it has to give the listener some instant gratification.

Into this slips chat. Something women do quite well. Jane's right, though: if you looked around in those dusty days of the early Wild West of podcasting it was only male chat. Big old slap on the back, head for the punchline, bro banter. The early successful podcasts were like codpieces of broadcasting. Have you seen the size of my punchline?

Ho. Ho. Ho.

Yet if you look around any bar or pub of an evening, the table with a group of women on it – especially 'midlife' women – has a rolling cackle of laughter as its soundtrack. It's noisy. Busy. Funny. I bet the humour is providing a current so strong it can carry any vessel of emotion along with it. Conversational multi-tasking is taking place. Someone is passing on the number of a good therapist or lawyer while also forwarding a link to a really cracking Matt Hancock meme. Lots of things will just get said and we'll all be happier for it. Better an empty house than bad tenants, as my mother always used to say. And half the population talks this way anyway.

But there wasn't a commotion and a rush to put all that wonderful female sound on the podcast airways because . . . well, actually, why wasn't there? I suspect it's for the same simple reason that enables all forms of the patriarchy. A belief that true north points to men. Broadcasting was a man's world for such a very long time. Most women had to ape male behaviour in order to get to the top, or just to get on air. Be assertive, perhaps even sometimes aggressive, or perch on the wire and chirrup when called upon. And because most men don't stay in the room when it's just women talking – or aren't invited in the first place – I suppose you could be generous and say it all sounded too odd and discombobulated to be considered valuable.

Some did try.

Ryan Dilley is the senior producer you are referring to, Jane. The one with the moustache. I know, I know, they all look the same. He was charged with getting Radio 4's 'digital offering' up and running. It is actually called that. It always makes me think of altars and collection plates, which is a bit weird. He asked us to do a pilot where we talked about things we had learned from each other, a kind of 'life hacks' thing. Apparently, when this was played to the powers-that-be they were aghast at the content. Aghast is the actual word that was used. I can't honestly remember what we talked about, but I know that it veered from sex to politics, with probably – knowing you – some kind of larder/crockery/pet anecdote in the middle. It went nowhere. Ryan left the BBC shortly afterwards to go and work with more successful pod-casters. I believe his offering is going well.

It took Rhian Roberts – woman, no moustache – to set us on the *Fortunately* path. As Radio 4's digital commissioner she has fought hard for us along the way. She is the one who tasked us with doing the radio review thingy, which I rather enjoyed. Being paid to listen to stuff I'd happily listen to anyway seemed like a gift from those same gods of broadcasting. But you are right that we seemed to stretch out beyond that pretty quickly to a more All Bar One menu of . . . er . . . pretty much anything at all. Huge credit to Roberts for allowing us to change tack. I suspect that she has sat in quite a few meetings where the notion of two midlife women discussing 'stuff' has been greeted with the same look that might pass over the faces of the assembled middle-management team if someone let go of the troubling wind that comes with too many of your Mexican bean wraps from the free buffet tray.

But hey, look, it turns out that women talking to women, not necessarily about women, is really quite popular. Thanks to our subscribers, we have become one of BBC Sounds' biggest podcasts and at the time of writing have 20 million downloads. I believe we got a mention in the BBC Annual Report, although it took a male listener to point this out to us in an email. And, yes, I have had to dig quite deep not to dress that achievement up in more modest, self-deprecating ribbons. Or apologise for drawing your attention to it.

But we definitely shouldn't say sorry for the fact that our podcast has been just wonderfully good fun. Jon Snow sang 'I Believe I Can Fly' to us, Kirsty Wark let us feel her broken nose, Clara Amfo chastised our lack of moisturising technique, Greg James revealed a love of self-tan, Will Self got stroppy, Nicky Campbell showed us his toe. At least we think that's what it was, we were on Zoom by then. Oh bloody Zoom. What is there left to say about that?

The pandemic brought with it such a sense of claustro-phobia and sadness and frustration and just unease, but there has not been a single week when I haven't looked forward to our self-help group of two, with eavesdroppers, to help make sense of our situation. Audio – as we now have to call it – has been one of the success stories in this horrible world of pain. It comes as no surprise: podcasts carry company and conversation as well as knowledge and expertise. And let's be honest, *Fortunately* is cheap, too. If you pay your licence fee, dear listener, then I think we cost you about 0.001p per year.

And when I say dear listener, I do really mean that, because it is our listeners who tickle our fancy the most. I know that sometimes it can sound sucky-uppy to say that, but I mean it most sincerely. And if we never had another guest again, or we could have the listeners as guests, I wouldn't mind at all. The email inbox suggests we'd never run out of things to talk about.

We have heard from women whose mothers have told them they regret having had them. Men who haven't been able to say they wanted kids. We've considered which hob ring is our favourite and pondered why the Teasmade didn't take off like the Nespresso machine. Are you Team Meghan and Harry or Team 'The Firm'? Would you like to tell us about your strange school trips, or the legendary problems of Cutlery Chuff? Do you also have a backward-facing cervix (me) or is your placenta in a museum (Jane)? We have heard about the horrendous caring demands so many people have placed upon them, shared in the loss of pets, congratulated people on completing marathons and chemotherapy courses. Our listeners' stories veer from the profound to the profane, just like real life does. We read every email and are better people for it.

It can be a really horrible world out there for women in broadcasting. Trolling. Shouting down. Abuse. Sexism. Just plain ghastly lasciviousness. But podcast listeners have to subscribe. They choose to be with us. And although, in our ever-decreasing silo society there is a massive need to stay listening to stuff you don't agree with, you also have a total right to listen to stuff that you do. I hope we provide something of a warmer embrace than a lot of the shoutier voices out there.

So. That is all the self-congratulatory good stuff. Enough. There are obvious pitfalls to two women making a podcast together. Because we are women, I'd expect us to be falling out sometime soon. We're over-due an absolute barnstormer of a row. Maybe with an ineffective fist fight and some hair-pulling? Definitely in the street. Maybe outside my private members' club or perhaps by the pool at your Lake Como summer retreat (is it deuce yet?). Then we can both sell our stories to the tabloids, maybe end up in court and then get a proper job once again alongside a less emotional man.

I'm joking. I hope this malarkey goes on for a very long time.

So, as you never, ever have to say on a podcast, but you do eventually have to say in a book, '. . . that's all we have time for. Goodbye.'

ACKNOWLEDGEMENTS

We'd like to say a sincere thank you to all the producers who've worked on the Fortunately podcast over the last four years, and have saved our bacon (insert vegan alternative) through their editing and expertise: Georgia Catt, Viv Jones, JP Devlin and Sam Peach. And an enormous thank you to Rhian Roberts at the BBC for getting it up and running in the first place; to Victoria Hobbs at AM Heath for persistently prodding us to write, and to Pippa Wright and the team at Orion for making it all possible.

CREDITS

Trapeze would like to thank everyone at Orion who worked on the publication of *Did I Say That Out Loud?*

Agent
Victoria Hobbs

Editor
Pippa Wright

Copy-editor
Linden Lawson

Proofreader
Abi Waters

Editorial Management
Sarah Fortune
Jane Hughes
Charlie Panayiotou

Tamara Morriss
Claire Boyle

Audio
Paul Stark
Jake Alderson

Contracts
Anne Goddard

Design
Rabab Adams
Joanna Ridley
Helen Ewing
Clare Sivell

Finance
Nick Gibson
Jasdip Nandra
Rabale Mustafa
Elizabeth Beaumont
Ibukun Ademefun
Afeera Ahmed
Levancia Clarendon
Tom Costello

Marketing
Helena Fouracre

Production
Nicole Abel
Fiona McIntosh

Publicity
Virginia Woolstencroft

Sales
Jen Wilson
Victoria Laws
Esther Waters
Frances Doyle
Ben Goddard
Georgina Cutler
Jack Hallam

Anna Egelstaff
Inês Figueira
Barbara Ronan
Andrew Hally
Dominic Smith
Deborah Deyong
Lauren Buck
Maggy Park
Linda McGregor
Sinead White
Jemimah James
Rachael Jones
Ian Williamson
Declan Kyle
Megan Smith
Rebecca Cobbold

Operations
Jo Jacobs
Sharon Willis

Rights
Susan Howe
Krystyna Kujawinska
Jessica Purdue
Ayesha Kinley
Louise Henderson